ho

Za

Introduction

In the name of Allah, the Entirely Merciful, the Especially Merciful.

Assalamu alaykum wa rahmatullahi wa barakatuh the purpose of writing 'Hot Coals' was to combine poetry and Islamic knowledge, related to the topic being discussed, in an easy to read, compact style.

I pray it proves to be an enjoyable and beneficial read and fills the reader's heart with the love of Allah (SWT) and the love of His Messenger (PBUH).

If you are reading this, I humbly request that you spare a few minutes to pray for the souls of my dear grandparents, who I lost recently.

They encouraged Islamic literature, instilled love for Allah and His Messenger (PBUH) in their children and grandchildren, and had a love for writing and meaningful poetry. May Allah (SWT) reward them for the good tarbiyah they gave us and may their graves be filled with light, space and smells of Jannah.

May Allah be pleased with them and may He be pleased with you all.

Allahumma Ameen.

Chapter 1

This World

This world is full of fitnah, deceit and lies,
Live in it as a traveller, if you are wise.

Don't be afraid to walk alone, Allah is near,
you're never on your own.

The path may seem long and weary to tread, But don't fret,
you'll find the road of goodness ahead.

You're surrounded by desires trying to destroy your soul,
Focus, and it'll be easier to attain Jannah, your goal!

I leave you with this message, a small reminder
for you and myself,
Let's strive to please Allah, our Creator,
let's focus on bettering our self.

Dunya vs. Aakhirah

My dear brothers and sisters in Islam...
Our time in this life is limited. We have a few years in this Dunya and then we will move on to a life which is forever. Allah (SWT) has repeatedly told us in the Qur'an, that the value of this life in comparison to the Aakhirah is very miniscule.

However, we live this short life, often forgetting about our life which will be forever; the afterlife. A single breath we take isn't guaranteed, and yet we busy ourselves preparing for our future in the World, rather than preparing for our Aakhira.

There are so many verses in the Qur'an that make comparisons between the worldly life and the Hereafter, the priority and emphasis always being on the Hereafter!

Allah (SWT) says in the Qur'an:

"O you who have believed, what is [the matter] with you that, when you are told to go forth in the cause of Allah, you adhere heavily to the Earth? Are you satisfied with the life of this world rather than the Hereafter? But what is the enjoyment of worldly life compared to the Hereafter except a [very] little."
(Surah At-Tawbah; 9:38)

Imam Ahmed recorded that Al-Mustawrid, a member of Bani Fihr, said that the Prophet (PBUH) said:

"The life of this world compared to the Hereafter, is just like when one of you dips his finger in the sea, let him contemplate how much of it his finger would carry."
(Sahih Muslim, Grade: Sahih)

In other places Allah (SWT) states:

"Allah extends provision for whom He wills and restricts [it].. And they rejoice in the worldly life, while the worldly life is not, compared to the Hereafter, except [brief] enjoyment."
(Surah Ar-Ra'd; 13:26)

"O mankind! Indeed the promise of Allah is truth, so let not the worldly life delude you and be not deceived about Allah, by the deceiver."
(Surah Fatir; 35:5)

"So let not the worldly life delude you" means; this life is nothing in comparison to the great good that Allah has promised to his close friends and the followers of his messengers. Do not let these transi-ent attractions distract you from that which is lasting.
(Tafsir ibn Kathir Surah Fatir verse 5)

Often we find ourselves lost in trying to gather as many worldly possessions as we can to help make our lives as comfortable as possible in the Dunya. We do this whilst neglecting our main goal and responsibility of preparing for our Aakhirah.

Everyone is in a race to surpass each other in materialistic possessions. Greedy to gain as much as possible from the Dunya, and as a result forgetting and neglecting the main purpose of life. The more you chase the Dunya, the more it runs away, until chasing it becomes an unsatisfactory addiction.

A true Muslim should consider this life as short term, and prepare for the eternal life in the Hereafter, which will bring ulti-mate success and contentment.

"And the worldly life is not but amusement and diversion; but the home of the Hereafter is best for those who fear Allah, so will you not reason?"

(Surah Al-An'am; 6:32)

These Ayah should motivate us to:

- To work towards the Aakhirah and not focus solely on the affairs of the Dunya
- To prioritise Deen over the Dunya
- Increase in good deeds and fear Allah
- To always remember that this life is fleeting and worth-less in the eyes of Allah
- Live this life according to the Qur'an and Sunnah and keep ourselves from falling into the tricks of Shaytaan (The Accursed).

Shaytaan tries his hardest to keep us distracted from our main purpose and goal in life. We must refrain from falling into his traps and stay focused on our goal of gaining Allah's pleasure and reaching the most beautiful destination; Jannah.

We have been granted 24 hours each day. How many of them hours do we spend working for some worldly gain and how many do we spend trying to please our Creator? Ponder upon that.

Dedicating more time for the sake of Allah, and fixing our int-en-tions should be our main priority.

Allah says in the Qur'an; "Mankind was created weak", how-ever He gives strength to His Believers, to overcome the temp-tations of Shaytaan.

The believer's life, life goals, time, effort, work and wealth should not be spent for this worldly life alone. They should be guid-ed by the desire to reach Jannah; the eternal abode of pleasure in the Hereafter.

The Messenger of Allah (PBUH) reminded us on numerous occasions, that this Dunya is worth nothing.

Ahadith Regarding the Insignificance of this Worldly Life:

Sahl bin Sa'd narrated that the Messenger of Allah (PBUH) said:

"If the world to Allah were equal to a mosquito's wing, then He would not allow the disbeliever to have a sip of water from it."

(Jami At-Tirmidhi, Grade: Hasan)

In another hadith RasulAllah sallallahu alayhi wasallam said:

"The life of this world compared to the Hereafter, is as if one of you were to put his finger in the ocean and take it out again, then compare the water that remains on his finger to the water that remains in the ocean."
(Sahih Muslim)

The first hadith means, whatever good things of the world Allah has given to those who deny His attribute of Oneness, as well as the Prophethood of His beloved Messenger, He has given those things to them because the world, as a whole, is entirely insignificant and valueless before Him.

On the authority of Ibn Umar (RAA):
The Messenger of Allah (PBUH) took me by the shoulder and said:

"Be in this world as though you were a stranger or a
Ibn Umar (RAA) used to say:

"When evening comes, do not expect to live till morning and when morning comes, do not expect to live till evening. Take from your health (a preparation) for your illness, and from your life for your death."
(Bukhari)

"Took me by the Shoulder and said..."

The fact that the Messenger sallallahu alayhi wasallam held Ibn Umar by the shoulder, demonstrates just how important the message was that he was going to give, as he wanted Ibn Umar's full attention, and wanted him to memorise what he was going to say.

To be as a Stranger

The stranger is usually prepared to eventually go back to his original home. He doesn't look like the people in his current en-vironment. He looks out of place, like a lion would amongst sheep.

Similarly, a believer should look different to those around him, who have taken this world as their main concern.

The believer's way of life, manner of speaking and dress should be different to the disbelievers. Those who have taken this world to be their home are consumed by it, where as the believer does not busy him/herself with it.

The stranger feels like he doesn't belong. His heart and mind are occupied with getting back to his home.

Likewise, the believer craves Allah's pleasure and his urgent desire is to reach the everlasting home of Paradise.

His heart and mind are occupied with reaching his final abode. Bear in mind, the believer isn't a stranger in a negative sense, rather they contribute to the good of this world, hoping for reward in the Hereafter.

To be as a Traveller

The traveller is always travelling, day and night to reach his destination. A stranger might keep more things than he needs, but a traveller takes as little as possible in terms of luggage and other things.
Similarly a believer should not be weighed down by materialistic things and shouldn't hoard the wealth and properties of Dunya, as if they are the most vital and important things.

The traveller has a guide, a map, or a GPS, which shows him the way to his destination and helps him reach it without getting lost.
Likewise, the believer has the Qur'an and Hadith, and scholarly guidance, which all work together to help explain exactly what to do and what not to do, in order to reach the final destination of Jannah.

To live life as a stranger is good, but to live life as a traveller is even better. This is because the stranger can settle in the land but the traveller is always moving, knowing that they cannot remain.

"This world is a bridge and a bridge should not be taken as a home."

Sayings of the Righteous Predecessors on Living Life as a Stranger or a Traveller

Al Hasan-al-Basri rahimahullah said:

"The believer is in the world like a stranger. He does not become unhappy from it's humiliation, nor does he compete for it's honour. He has one purpose and the people have another purpose."
(Jaami' al-'Uloom wal-Hikam)

Imaam An-Nawawi rahimahullah stated:

"A person in this world is like a slave who was sent by his master to another land, to fulfil some objective. His goal will be to fulfil that objective as quickly as possible, and then return to his land and owner. As long as he is there, he will not bother with anything else along the way or with gathering as much as he can from that other land."
(Imaam an-Nawawi rahimahullah was quoted by ibn Hajr rahimahullah Fath al-Tijaariyyah)

Ibn Qayyim Al Jawziyya said:

"O people who take pleasure in a life that will vanish, falling in love with a faded shadow is sheer stupidity!"

Abu Ad Darda said:

"He who feels that he is in need of this life, then he has no life."
(Hilyatul-Awliya)

Imaam Ibn Hajr rahimahullah stated:

"In the same way that a traveller is not in need of more than what will get him to his destination, a believer does not need any more of this world than what will help him reach his [desired] destination [of Paradise]."
(Fath al-Tijaariyyah)

How to use this Life to Gain Success in the Hereafter

We have been put on this world to live our due share, so we cannot escape from it and we can't ignore the challenges it poses or the difficulties we may face along the way. Islam does not expect us to completely withdraw ourselves and live a life of complete soli-tude. A believer uses the Dunya, to benefit his Deen.

We are supposed to live life, utilising all the resources Allah The Most Generous, has bestowed upon us.

Allah tells us in the Qur'an,

"But seek, through that which Allah has given you, the home of the Hereafter; and [yet], do not forget your share of the world. And do good as Allah has done good to you. And desire not corruption in the land. Indeed, Allah does not like corrupters."

(Surah Al Qasas, 28:77)

So how can a believer maintain a steady balance between living life and preparing for eternal success in the Hereafter?

Start Mentally Thinking of Yourself as a Stranger

Train yourself to see every situation as a passing one. Nothing lasts forever in the Dunya. No matter how much wealth you have, you wont be taking it with you to the Hereafter, you'll be entering your grave alone. Remember that!

You have 3 stages in life:

1. Your time in the womb
2. Your life in this world
3. Everlasting Hereafter

The first stage has already passed, you're currently living the second and the third and most important stage is nearby. Prepare yourself.

Don't Chase After the World

Don't stress and worry yourself about worldly matters. Place your trust in Allah and know that as long as you focus on the Hereafter and make it your priority, all your worldly matters will be sorted, bi-idhnillah.
Tawakkul ala Allah

Umar (radi Allahu anhu) said: "I heard the Messenger of Allah (PBUH) say:

"If you were to rely upon Allah with the reliance He is due, you would be given provision like the birds: They go out hungry in the morning and come back with full bellies in the evening."
(Ibn Majah - graded hasan, Tirmidhi)

Ibn Qayyim Al-Jawziyyah said:

"This dunya (world) is like a shadow. If you try to catch it, you will never be able to do so. If you turn your back towards it, it has no choice but to follow you."

MAKE A TIMETABLE

Plan your day around Salah, not Salah around your day. Make the conscious effort to prioritise Deen over Dunya in your day to day life. This way you will be able to keep track on how much time you spend in preparation for the Hereafter and aim to do better daily.

PRACTISE MINIMALISM

Try only buying what you actually need, rather than what you want. Start removing the non essentials from your home and your belongings. Give what you don't need to charity. The more you give in charity, the more your heart grows in generosity and the more excess is removed from your life, the more humility grows inside of you.

PRAY

Make dua that Allah (SWT) makes this journey easy
for you and rewards you for the struggles you may face. Ask for His Help to keep you steadfast and focused on the straight path of righteousness and that the temptations of this world cower away from you.
Ameen

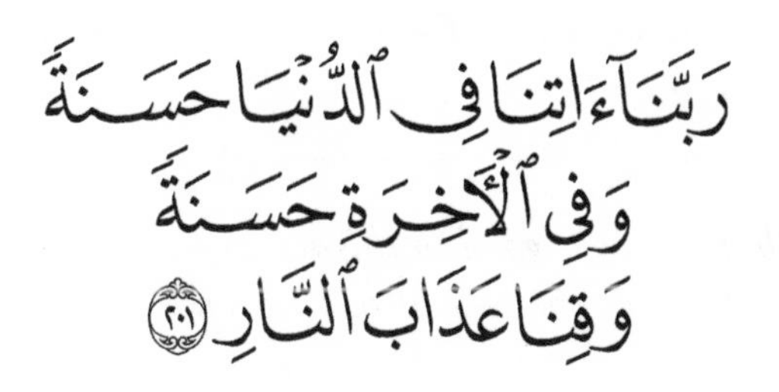

The Prophet Muhammad (PBUH) was lying on a hard mat. Ibn Mas'ud (radi Allahu anhu) began to wipe the effects of the mat from the Prophet (PBUH)' s blessed body and suggested that he have something better to sleep on. The Prophet (PBUH) replied:

"What do I have to do with this worldly life? I and this world are but like a traveller who stopped for a little while under a tree to get some shade and then he moved on."
(Recorded by Imam Ahmad, At-Tirmidhi, Ibn Majah + others)

Yahya Bin Mu'adh said:

"The night is long, so do not make it shorter by excessive sleeping. The day is pure, so do not stain it by your sins. Be like a passerby in this life, realizing that leaving comes after a little rest and that moving along comes faster than the respite."

My brothers and sisters, be honest with yourself and try to always uti-lise this world to gain nearness to Allah and to seek His Pleasure. May Allah grant us all hearts that pull towards good, and actions that will weigh heavily on our right scale. Allahumma Ameen

---

Contribute what is good to this world but don't work for the sake of this world!

Chapter 2

"And my loved ones walked away"

I lived my life, forgetting death,
Chasing the Dunya, till my very last breath.
I prayed, Yes! I fasted too,
But not enough, deep down I always knew,
There was so much more that I could do,
I had so many chances, myself I threw.

Now my life flashed in front of my hollow eyes,
As I waited for my punishment or prize.
I could hear them alive, standing over me,
Shovelling the last heaps of soil on top of me.
I was voiceless but screaming, "Don't leave me, please stay"
But my loved ones couldn't hear me and they walked away.

Was I to be tormented or blessed?
Had I failed or passed my test?
Would my grave prove to be a fiery pit of hell?
Or breezy sweet scents from Jannah would I smell?
Did I live my life, striving to please my Creator?
Or were the worldly temptations for me, much greater?

Time was up! I was left with the good and
bad deeds I had sowed,
Death was not the end. It was just the
beginning of a long, long road.
I wished my family would stay, I wished I could pray,
But in the end, my loved ones walked away.

REALITY OF DEATH

Generations upon generations of men and women have walked upon this Earth. Not a single one could escape the reality of death. Many have been arrogant and ignorant and convinced themselves that they could evade it, but No! Life is like a dream and death is the wake up call.

No one has the power to avoid it, nor does anyone around the dying person have the ability to prevent it.

It is something, which happens every moment and is encountered by the old and the young, the rich and the poor, the strong and the weak.

Every single human being who was born in the world has two things in common:

1. All are delivered from their mother's womb
2. All will taste death

A believer must remember that death is inevitable. It can reach anyone at any time and any place. Only Allah (SWT) Knows when and where. Even the Angel of Death himself does not have knowledge of the time of a person's death prior to Allah's command.

Imam Ahmad mentions in al-Zuhd as well as Ibn Abi al-Dunya from Ma`mar who said:

"It reached us that the Angel of death does not have knowledge of when a person's lifespan will end until he is commanded to take [the soul]."

(Al-Suyuti, al-Haba'ik fi Akhbar al-Mala'ik)

We have been given the knowledge through the Quran and ahadith, as to what exactly happens before, during and after death. It is just the timing of death which we have no knowledge of.
It is a natural occurrence, merely marking a transition between the material world and that of the unseen, leading to the Hereafter.

Signs of death can be seen all around. When a believer attends a funeral and when members of family and friends die, it is a reminder that they themselves could be next.
When the leaves are shed from trees and trees are left bare, it is a reminder that nothing in the Dunya will last forever.
Everything will whither and die.

Though death is certain, and we are surrounded by so many signs and reminders we still tend to forget from time to time our meeting with our Lord. All life belongs to Allah, and to Him we will all return.
Death is the reality from which none can escape and our grave is our true home until we reach the Hereafter. Remember that always.

Allah (SWT) states in the Glorious Qur'an:

"Every soul will taste death, and you will only be given your [full] compensation on the Day of Resurrection. So he who is drawn away from the Fire and admitted to Paradise has attained [his desire]. And what is the life of this world except the enjoyment of delusion"
(Surah Al-Imran, 3:185)

"Wherever you may be, death will overtake you, even if you should be within towers of lofty construction"...
(Surah An-Nisa, 4:78)

"*Every soul will taste death*" is a clear cut promise from Allah and nothing can go against it.
"And what is this life except the enjoyment of delusion" Allah has described life as the enjoyment of delusion because people become so engrossed in enjoying their life that they forget about their true purpose, and they forget about death.

"And it is not [possible] for one to die except by permission of Allah at a decree determined. And whoever desires the reward of this world - We will give him thereof; and whoever desires the reward of the Hereafter - We will give him thereof. And we will reward the grateful."
(Surah Al-Imran, 3:145)

"Every soul will taste death. Then to Us will you be returned."
(Surah Al-'Ankabut, 29:57)

The verses mentioned here about death, are a constant reminder for those who pay heed. Indeed we all will die!
The reminder of death is there so that we live our life accordingly. When we realise that death is around the corner and can take us at anytime, we become more mindful of our actions and try our hardest to become better versions of ourselves.

"When we are born, adhaan is given
When we die, salah is prayed
That's how short life is;
The time between adhaan and salah"

Ahadith Regarding Death:

Abu Hurayra (radi Allahu anhu) reported that the Messenger of Allah, (PBUH) said:

"Remember frequently the thing that cuts off pleasures," i.e. death."
(At-Tirmidhi)

In another narration, the prophet (PBUH) said:

"Remember often the destroyer of pleasures. Never does a servant remember it during hardship except that it will become easier for him, and never does he not remember it during ease except that it will become harder for him."
(Sahih Ibn Hibban, Grade: Hasan)

A believer should never fear death, rather he/she should remember it often and reflect upon the purpose of life.
Remember, death is merely a passing from this world on to the next.
The more you think of it, the more serious your outlook towards

life becomes and the world and it's pleasures begin to seem very insignifi-cant. Think about all the loved ones you have buried beneath the soil and how they are no longer remembered and all traces of them have dis-appeared. This will help you to focus more on preparing for your death and doing good deeds that will help you in your grave.
Remembering death also helps to soften the heart.

Imam Qurtubi (rahimahu Allah) related that the scholars said:

"Remembering death deters one from sin, softens the hard heart, stops one from delighting in this world, and makes disasters look bearable."

It is narrated that a woman complained to 'Aa'ishah (radi Allahu anha) of the hardness in her heart. She said to her:

"Remember death often, for that will soften your heart."

(She did that, and her heart was softened)
Qurtubi

Moment of Death

When the appointed time comes and a person's life is drawing to a close, Allah (SWT) sends the messengers of death to bring forth the soul from the body of His servant.
The Angels of Death come to the believers in a beautiful form, and they come to the disbelievers in a frightening form.
It is in this moment that each person will know that their time

on this Dunya has come to an end.
The agonies of death are the last hardship that a person encounters before meeting Allah, and they are the last thing by means of which Allah expiates the sins of His slave. We ask Allah to make these agonies easy for us and help us to bear them. Ameen

"And He is the subjugator over His servants, and He sends over you guardian-angels until, when death comes to one of you, Our messengers take him, and they do not fail [in their duties]."
(Surah Al-An'aam, 6:61)

A Believer's Death

Usually if a believer has lived his/her life striving to please Allah (SWT), he/she welcomes death upon seeing the angels, for which believer does not wish to reach Allah.
The true servant of Allah embraces death like a mother embraces her child. For a believer, who has feared Allah during life, lived according to the Quran and Sunnah, and taken care of his/her Deen related affairs, death is a relief. One part of their journey has come to an end, and the next is just a waiting stop, till they reach their eternal abode in Jannah.

Many of the salaf, wept when death reached them, however their tears weren't out of fear of death, rather they fell in sorrow for the cessation of their righteous deeds.

The death of the believer is a beautiful affair.

Allah (SWT) says in the Holy Qur'an:

"Indeed, those who have said, "Our Lord is Allah" and then remained on a right course - the angels will descend upon them, [saying], "Do not fear and do not grieve but receive good tidings of Par-adise, which you were promised."

(Surah Fussilat, 41:30)

"[To the righteous it will be said],
"O reassured soul,
Return to your Lord, well-pleased and pleasing [to Him],
And enter among My [righteous] servants
And enter My Paradise."

(Surah Al-Fajr, 89:27-30)

Abdullah Ibn Masud said:

"In the morning, the believers thank Allah for survival; and after death, they are thankful for their Taqwa."

A Muslim has nothing to fear from death.
If a person spends his life doing good (with sincerity), in sha Allah, his death will come on goodness. It is a blessing of Allah because he will be resurrected in the Hereafter in the state of what he was doing when death came to him. Therefore, we should spend more and more time in doing righteous work.
Narrated Abdullah ibn Amr: Allah's Messenger (PBUH) said, *"The gift to a believer is death."*

Hadith about a Believer's Death

Imam Ahmad recorded that Al-Bara bin `Azib said: "We went with the Messenger of Allah to attend a funeral procession of an Ansari man. We reached the grave site when it had not yet been completed.
The Messenger of Allah (PBUH) sat, and we all sat all around him, as if there were birds hovering above our heads.

The Prophet (PBUH) was holding a piece of wood in his hand, poking the ground with it. He next raised his head and said twice or thrice:

"I Seek refuge with Allah from the punishment of the grave."

He (PBUH) said next,

"When a believing slave is reaching the end of his term in the life of this world and the beginning of his term in the Hereafter, a group of angels, whose faces are white and as radiant as the sun, will descend onto him from heaven. They will carry with them white shroud from Paradise, and fragrance for enshrouding from Paradise. They will sit as far from him as the sight goes. Then, the angel of death, will come until he sits right next to his head, saying, "O, good and pure soul! Depart (your body) to Allah's forgiveness and pleasure." So the soul flows (out of its body), just as the drop flows out from the tip of the jug, and the angel of death captures it. When he captures the soul, they (the group of angels) will not leave it with him for more than an instance, and they will seize it and

wrap it in that shroud, and in that fragrance. A most pleasant musk scent ever found on the earth, will flow out of the soul, and the angels will ascend it (to heaven). They will not pass by, but they will say, "Whose is this Tayyib (good) soul" They (the angels who are ascending the soul) will reply, "Such person, the son of such and such person," -- calling him by the best names that he used to be called in the world. They will reach the lower heaven and will ask that its door be opened for him, and it will be opened for them. The best residents of every heaven will then see him to the next heaven, until he is brought to the seventh heaven. Allah, the Exalted and Ever High, will say, "List my servants record in `Illiyyin and send him back to earth, for I have created them from it, and into it I shall return them, and from it I shall bring them out once again." The soul will be joined with its body, and two angels will come to him, sit him up and ask him, "Who is your Lord" He will say, "Allah is my Lord." They will ask him, "What is your religion" He will say, "My religion is Islam." They will say to him, "What do you say about this man (Prophet Muhammad) who was sent to you" He will say, "He is the Messenger of Allah." They will ask him, "And what proof do you have about it" He will say, "I read the Book of Allah (the Qur'an), and had faith and belief in him." Then, a caller (Allah) will herald from heaven, "My servant has said the truth. Therefore, furnish him from Paradise, and let him wear from (the clothes of) Paradise, and open a door for him to Paradise." So he is given from Paradise's tranquillity and good scent, and his grave will be expanded for *him as far as his sight can reach. Then, a man, with a handsome face and handsome clothes and whose scent is pleasant, will come to him, saying, "Receive the glad tidings with that which pleases you. This is the Day which you were promised." He will ask him, "Who are you; for yours is the face that carries the good news" He will reply, "I am your good works." He will say, "O Lord! Hurry up with the commencement of the Hour, hurry up with the commencement of the Hour, so I can return to my family and my wealth."*

A Disbeliever's Death

A person who spent his/her life in disbelief will have a most horrifying death. They will panic upon seeing the angels of death and will be filled with regret and pain.
They will dread meeting Allah, for they know they disobeyed Him all their life.
They will beg to be given another chance even though they were blessed with a lifetime of health to obey Allah as He ought to be obeyed. Once death appears it is much too late.

Allah (SWT) says in the Holy Qur'an:

"[For such is the state of the disbelievers], until, when death comes to one of them, he says, "My Lord, send me back, That I might do righteousness in that which I left behind." No! It is only a word he is saying; and behind them is a barrier until the Day they are resurrected."
(Surah Al-Mu'minoon, 23:99-100)

Throughout their life, they were given reminders of the truth, yet they turned a deaf ear. When they see the harsh reality of death and the truth is in front of them, they will suffer from severe grief. They know that they themselves are to blame. They chose to live how they did and disregarded all the signs around them, so they could carry on in their heedlessness, doing as they pleased.

When death reaches them it will be too late and their souls will be taken with great suffering and difficulty. A'udhu'billah

"Then how [will it be] when the angels take them in death, striking their faces and their backs?"
(Surah Muhammad, 47:27)

"And if you could but see when the wrongdoers are in the overwhelming pangs of death while the angels extend their hands, [saying], "Discharge your souls! Today you will be awarded the punishment of [extreme] humiliation for what you used to say against Allah other than the truth and [that] you were, toward His verses, being arrogant."
(Surah Al-An'am, 6:93)

It is impossible to fully comprehend what disbelievers experience at the time of death. However, Allah depicts this situation so that we can contemplate and avoid meeting such an end.

The angels of death, as the verses suggest, will take the souls of disbelievers while smiting their faces and their backs.

By that moment, disbelievers will suffer physical pain accompanied by a deep regret since they will know they no longer have an
opportunity to return back.

(Continuing from the hadith of Al-Bara bin `Azib)

"And when the disbelieving person is reaching the end of his term in the world and the beginning of his term in the Hereafter, there will descend onto him from heaven angels with dark faces. They will bring with them Musuh, and will sit as far from him as the sight reaches. Then the angel of death will come forward and sit right next to his head, saying, "O impure, evil soul! Depart (your body) to the anger of Allah and a wrath from Him." The soul will scatter throughout his body, and the angel of death will seize it as when the thorny branch is removed from wet wool. The angel of death will seize the soul, and when he does, they (the group of angels) will not let it stay in his hand for more than an instance, and they will wrap it in the Musuh. The most putrid smell a dead corpse can ever have on earth will emit from the soul, and the angels will ascend with it.
Whenever they pass by a group of angels, they will ask, "Whose is this evil soul" The angels will respond, "He is such person son of such person," -- calling him by the worst names he was known by in the world.
When they reach the lowest heaven, they will request that its door be opened for him, and their request will be denied. "For them the gates of heaven will not be opened, and they will not enter Paradise until the camel goes

through the eye of the needle.
Allah will declare, "List his record in Sijjin in the lowest earth."
The wicked soul will then be thrown from heaven.
"And whoever assigns partners to Allah, it is as if he had fallen from the sky, and the birds had snatched him, or the wind had thrown him to a far off place." His soul will be returned to his body, and two angels will come to him, sit him up and ask him, "Who is your Lord" He will say, "Oh, oh! I do not know." They will ask him, "What is your religion", and he will say, "Oh, oh! I do not know." They will ask him, "What do you say about this man (Prophet Muhammad) who was sent to you" He will say, "Oh, oh, I do not know!" A caller (Allah) will herald from heaven, "My serv-ant has lied, so furnish him with the Fire and open a door for him to the Fire." He will find its heat and fierce hot wind. And his grave will be reduced in size, until his bones crush each other. Then, a man with a dreadful face, wearing dreadful clothes and with a disgusting smell emitting from him will come to him, saying, "Receive the glad tidings with that which will displease you! This is the Day that you have been promised." He will ask that man, "And who are you, for yours is the face that brings about evil" He will say, "I am your evil work." He will therefore cry, "O, my Lord! Do not commence the Hour!"

The Angel Of Death

There are 4 arch angels. The angel of death known as Malak ul maut, is one of the four main most respected angels.

Commonly known as Azra'il, however he is only mentioned in authentic hadith as Malakul maut.
It is noted that The Angel of Death will look like a terrifying beast or demon for the souls of bad people and will look like 'the most pleasant sight' when he comes for the souls of good people.

Allah (SWT) says in the Holy Qur'an:

"Say, The angel of death will take you who has been entrusted with you. Then to your Lord you will be returned."

(Surah As-Sajdah, 32:11)

Malak ul Maut and Prophet Musa Alayhis-Salaam

Narrated Abu Huraira:

The angel of death was sent to Moses and when he went to him, Moses slapped him severely, spoiling one of his eyes. The angel went back to his Lord, and said, "You sent me to a slave who does not want to die." Allah restored his eye and said, "Go back and tell him (i.e. Moses) to place his hand over the back of an ox, for he will be allowed to live for a number of years equal to the number of hairs coming under his hand." (So the angel came to him and told him the same). Then Moses asked, "O my Lord! What will be then?" He said, "Death will be then." He said, *"(Let it be) now...."*

(Sahih al-Bukhari)

Zuhri has narrated from Anas b. Malik that he said: "I heard the Messenger of Allah (PBUH) say,

'There is not a single house which exists except that the Angel of Death visits it five times a day. If the lives of any of the people who live in the house or those who are within the house are written to come to an end, then he brings death upon that person.
When the agonies and tribulations of death clothe the entire presence of the person; the screams of the people of the house increase; the people start to pull their hair and start to hit their head and face, and cry, it is at this time that the Angel of Death says, 'Fie be upon you! Why are you showing anger and fear?
I swear by Allah! I have not taken anyone's wealth; I have not brought the appointed time (of death) any closer and I have not come towards you without permission (from Allah). Rather, I am taking the soul by the permission of someone else (Allah). I will continue to come to this house until not a single person remains."

At this point the Prophet (PBUH) said,

"I swear by the One who holds my life and soul in His hands, if you were to see the station where the Angel of Death is standing in the house and were to hear his words, you would surely forget the one who has passed away! Rather, you would shed tears for yourself!
As the deceased is being carried in his casket, his spirit stays above the casket, crying out, 'O' my family! O' my children! Do not let the transient world play with you as

it played with me in which I collected the wealth both from the permissible and impermissible means and then left it for others behind me (to inherit). May felicity and delight be for those who have inherited that wealth, however, a responsibility remains on my shoulders. Be careful since that which has come upon me shall also come upon you."

The Grave

People compete in building the loftiest of houses in the Dunya, but eventually everyone is buried deep in soil.

The grave will be either one of the gardens of Paradise or one of the pits of Hell, depending on the faith and the nature of the deeds committed by the person. The torment or blessing will happen to the body as well as the soul in the grave, and also in the Hereafter, in either Paradise or Hell.

The soul remains in a place of limbo in it's grave, called the Barzakh, until the Day of Judgment.

Two frightening angels called *Munkar* and *Nakeer*, visit the soul to ask it about it's religion, God, and prophet. Only an honest believer will be able to answer these questions correctly, whereas, a disbeliever will fail in answering all of them and will face severe consequences.

The Prophet Muhammad (PBUH) said:

"When a deceased person is laid in his grave, he hears the sound of the footsteps of people as they go away. If he is a believer, the prayer will stand by his head, the fasting

will be to his right, alms to his left, and all other good deeds of charity, kindness to relations, and good behaviour will be by his feet."
(Ahmad)

MUNKAR AND NAKEER

Abu (radi Allahu anhu) Hurayrah narrated that the Messenger of Allah (PBUH) said:

"When the deceased is buried (or he said: when one of you is buried), there come to him two blue-black angels, one of whom is called Munkar and the other Nakeer. They ask him, 'What did you used to say about this man?' and he says what he used to say: 'He is the slave and Messenger of Allah: I bear witness that there is no god except Allah and that Muhammad is the slave and Messenger of Allah. They say, 'We knew beforehand that you used to say this.' Then his grave will be widened for him to a size of seventy cubits by seventy cubits and it will be illuminated for him. Then they tell him, 'Sleep.' He says, 'Go back to my family and tell them.' They tell him, 'Sleep like a bridegroom whom no-one will wake up except his most beloved,' until Allah raises him up. If (the deceased) was a hypocrite, he says, 'I heard the people saying something so I said something similar; I do not know.' They say: 'We knew beforehand that you used to say this.'

The earth will be told to squeeze him, so he will be crushed until his ribs are interlocked, and he will remain like that until Allah raises him up.'"

(At–Tirmidhi)

The thought of Munkar and Nakeer is quite frightening, however a believer has nothing to fear from them. They are the servants of Allah, just like you and I are. As a believing Muslim, if anything, you should welcome the questioning, as it is a chance to openly declare and bear witness to the testimony of faith.

The believer upon answering the questions correctly, will see his grave is made roomy and spacious and filled with light. He is shown what would have been his abode in Hell - had he been a wicked sinner - before a portal is opened for him every morning and evening showing him his actual home in Paradise.

O what a beautiful sight that would be!

However the disbeliever, upon not having an answer for the questions, will see the heat and hot wind of Hell come unto him, then his grave will be contracted upon him until his limbs are caught up among one another.

What a pitiful, horrifying sight! A'udhu'billah

Their condition will stay like this until Allah resurrects everyone on the Day of Judgement.

Seeking Allah's Protection

The Messenger of Allah (PBUH) said:

"Seek Allah's protection from the Punishment of the Grave, since punishment of the Grave is a fact/true."
(At-Tabbranee)

The punishment in the grave and in the Hereafter is an indication of the wrath of Allah upon His slave; The one who made Allah angry in this life and did not repent, and died while in that state will be punished in the grave.

The punishment of the grave is compensation for a person's sins in the world. We should always seek refuge with Allah (SWT) from the trial of the grave as the Prophet (PBUH) did.

Prophet Muhammad (PBUH) said:

"These people are being tortured in their graves, and were it not that you would stop burying your dead, I would ask Allah to let you hear the punishment in the grave...."
(Part of a hadith recorded in Sahih Muslim)

What can a Muslim do to Avoid the Punishment in the Grave?

Allah (SWT), through His Divine Mercy has granted us the knowledge of a few things that a believer can do that could protect him/her from any torment in the grave.

Read Surah Mulk

Reciting Surah Mulk at night is said to protect a person from punishment in the grave and a believer is encouraged to make a habit of reading it frequently.

Al-Mannaawi said :

"The Surah will give protection to the one who recited it; when he dies and is placed in his grave, he will not be punished there"

Narrrated from Abu Hurayrah (radi Allahu anhu) that the Prophet (PBUH) said:

"There is a surah of the Qur'an, with thirty verses, that interceded for a man until he was forgiven; it is 'Surah Tabaarak Alladhi bi yadihi'l-mulk (Blessed is He in Whose Hand is the dominion)' [al-Mulk 67:1]."

(Abu Dawood and At-Tirmidhi)

Increase in Worship

Remember Allah (SWT) at all times, increase in dhikr and worship and stay away from the things that Allah (SWT) has forbidden.

Remembering Allah and keeping your tongue fresh with dhikr and remembrance of Allah keeps the Shaytaan away, and in

turn helps protect you from committing sins and earning the wrath of Allah. Allah loves those who remember Him and forgives those who ask for His forgiveness. The more good you do, the more you protect yourself from sin and punishment in the grave.
Dhikr cleanses the soul of impurities, and you automatically gravitate towards doing good and in turn gain Allah's Mercy. The more deeds a Muslim does that are pleasing in the Sight of Allah (SWT), the more beautiful his/her affairs in the grave shall be.

Stay in a State of Purity

A believer should take extra care and make sure their clothes and body are pure and clean at all times. Being careless in regards to washing yourself is one of the causes of punishment in the grave.

Ibn Abbas (radi Allahu anhuma) says that the Messenger of Allah, (PBUH), once, while passing by two graves, remarked:

"The inmates of these two graves are being tortured not for any serious sins, but in fact they are serious sins. One of them used to carry tales and the other used not to wash when urinating."
(Bukhari and Muslim)

Stay away from both minor and major sins. Sometimes a person deems a sin as small and insignificant, but it could cause much harm in the grave.
The punishment in the grave is a compensation for a person's sins in the world. A believer is mostly punished in the grave so that he does not have to suffer on the Day of Judgment.

A minor sin can be erased through a good deed done after it, however a major sin can only be forgiven through seeking Allah's forgiveness and doing pure Tawbah.
In the above hadith, the prophet sallallahu alayhi wasallam said, "not for any serious sins, but in fact they are serious sins." This was said to show that people consider these sins as minuscule however they are serious.
A believer should always be precautious. May Allah grant us khayr.

Make Dua

Most importantly a believer must pray to Allah (SWT) that He protects him/her from the torment of the grave and forgives their sins. He is Most Just, Most Merciful, The overall Protector.

اللَّهُمَّ إِنِّي أَعُوذُ بِكَ مِنْ فِتْنَةِ النَّارِ وَعَذَابِ النَّارِ، وَفِتْنَةِ الْقَبْرِ، وَعَذَابِ الْقَبْرِ، وَشَرِّ فِتْنَةِ الْغِنَى، وَشَرِّ فِتْنَةِ الْفَقْرِ

O Allah! I seek refuge in you from the affliction of the Hell Fire and its torment, from the affliction of the grave and its torment,and from the evil of the affliction of wealth and poverty

(AL-Bukhari # 6377)

Allah (SWT) is the Only one who can Save us and Help us. Even if we only had good deeds on our scales, we can not benefit from them without the Mercy of Allah. Always ask for His Help and He can save us from any torment and any punishment in this life and in the next.

اللَّهُمَّ إِنِّي أَعُوذُ بِكَ عَذَابِ الْقَبْرِ، ومِنْ عَذابِ جَهَنَّمَ، وَمِن فِتْنَةِ المَحْيَا وَالمَمَاتِ، وَمِنْ شَرِّ فِتْنَةِ المَسِيحِ الدَّجَّالِ

O Allah! I seek refuge in You, from the punishment of the grave, and from the punishment of the Hell fire, and from the trials of life and death, and from the evil of the trial of the False Messiah

---

It is reported that Al-Hasan Al-Basrī – Allāh have mercy on him – once said during the funeral of a man:

"May Allāh have mercy on the man who works for the likes of this day; for today you are able to do what these brothers of yours, the residents of these graves, cannot do. So make full use of your health and free time before the day of dis-tress and accounts comes upon you."

"There is no comfort or rest for the believer until he/she meets Allah"

Chapter 3

His Mercy Outweighs His Wrath

Allah! The Creator of the heavens and the Earth,
The One with us, since before our mother's gave us birth.
He gave us life, so we would spend it in submission,
Every breath of air we take is only by His permission.
He blesses us and blesses us, in every single way,
Yet we remain ungrateful, sinning every single day.
He gives us chances upon chances, to sort ourselves out,
Gaining His pleasure, is what this life is all about.
Yes, we're human, our feet sometimes stray from his path,
But always remember, His Mercy outweighs His Wrath.
We have the Qur'an and the Sunnah,
in which there is no doubt,
O fellow Muslims, In His worship we need to be devout.

ALLAH'S MERCY

Allah (SWT) is the Most Merciful, Most Compassionate and Caring, Most Loving, Most Forgiving, and His Mercy encompasses all things.

Everything good in this world; all the blessings in this world and the next, are clear proofs of this.

Throughout life, people continually receive Allah's blessings, be it good health, sight, hearing, nourishment, children, wealth and countless others. It is through His Mercy that we receive these blessings.

Every single breath we take has been gifted to us by The Most Merciful from His Mercy. SubhanAllah.

Allah (SWT) says in the Holy Qur'an:

"My punishment - I afflict with it whom I will, but My mercy encompasses all things."
(Surah Al-A'raf, 7:156)

"Peace be upon you. Your Lord has decreed upon Himself mercy: that any of you who does wrong out of ignorance and then repents after that and corrects himself - indeed, He is Forgiving and Merciful."
(Surah Al-An'am, 6:54)

"Degrees [of high position] from Him and forgiveness and mercy. And Allah is ever Forgiving and Merciful."
(Surah An-Nisa, 4:96)

"Say, "O My servants who have transgressed against themselves [by sinning], do not despair of the mercy of Allah. Indeed, Allah forgives all sins. Indeed, it is He who is the Forgiving, the Merciful.
And return [in repentance] to your Lord and submit to Him before the punishment comes upon you; then you will not be helped."
(Surah Az-Zumar, 39:53-54)

AHADITH ON ALLAH'S MERCY

Abu Hurayra reported: I heard Allah's Messenger (PBUH) saying:

ah created mercy in one hundred parts and He re-
ned with Him ninety-nine parts, and He has sent
n upon the earth one part, and it is because of this
part that there is mutual love among the creation so
h so that the animal lifts up it's hoof from it's young
one, fearing that it might harm it."

(Sahih Muslim)

If only 1 part of Mercy has been given to all of creation, and 99 parts are with Allah, how can a person even begin to imagine the extent of Allah's Mercy?

We experience His Mercy every moment of our lives. We would be lost without it.

Animals, humans, and jinn, all who have lived, are living, and are yet to come, have a share in that one part of Mercy. It is through that portion of Mercy that people find it within themselves to forgive each other, a mother sacrifices everything for her child, and a father tires himself day and night to provide for his family. Ninety nine parts are with Allah alone, so how can we despair in His Mercy?

Abu Hurayra reported: I heard Allah's Messenger (PBUH) as saying:

"There are one hundred (parts of) mercy for Allah and

He has sent down out of these, one part of mercy upon the jinn and human beings and the insects and it is because of this (one part) that they love one another, show kindness to one another and even the beast treats it's young one with affection, and Allah has reserved ninety-nine parts of mercy with which He would treat His servants on the Day of Resurrection"

(Sahih Muslim)

If a person was to be asked about who loves them the most, they'd undoubtedly say, 'my mother'.

Look at a mother's mercy towards her child. No matter how difficult a child is, how much they refuse to listen and misbehave, a mother's love and mercy will never waver.

She never intends any harm unto her children and sacrifices all her needs for the needs of her offspring.

A mother's love and compassion for her child is one of the strongest, purest forms of mercy we experience.

Islamic teachings build on this experience to help us understand the love and mercy of Allah.

The Prophet Muhammad (PBUH) taught us that Allah's Mercy towards His believing slaves is greater than a mother's mercy towards her child, for as was stated in the previous ahadith, the mercy granted to Creation is nothing compared to the Mercy Allah (SWT) has reserved with Himself for His servants. With Allah (SWT) are 99 portions of Mercy; a number and an amount that no human mind can comprehend.

We make so many mistakes throughout our lives, and repeat them, however Allah still gives us an opportunity to change, to see the error of our ways, and to make a fresh start. All He asks is that we turn to Him and repent after every mistake.

How Merciful Allah is! SubhanAllah

Umar ibn Khattab (radi Allahu anhu) reported that there were brought some prisoners to Allah's Messenger (PBUH) amongst whom there was also a woman, who was searching (for someone) and when she found a child amongst the prisoners, she took hold of it, pressed it against her chest and provided it suck.

Thereupon Allah's Messenger (PBUH) said:

"Do you think this woman would ever afford to throw her child in the Fire?"

We said: *"By Allah, so far as it lies in her power, she would never throw the child in Fire."*

Thereupon Allah's Messenger said:

"Allah is more kind to His servants than this woman is to her child."

(Sahih Muslim)

Hence, a slave should never despair of the Mercy of Allah, The Almighty. Rather, whenever he/she commits a sin, they should ask for forgiveness and repent to Allah. No one is infallible. Every human no matter how righteous, falls in to sin. It is due to Allah's Mercy that we seek His Forgiveness.

The believer must remain in a state between hoping for the Mercy of Allah (SWT) and fearing His punishment.

The mercy of Allah is ever present. It is the believer who must learn how to tap into that mercy and learn to live their life in a way that will make them deserving of that mercy.

Acknowledging Allah's Rahma upon us, and knowing that He cares for and loves us and is always waiting for us to turn back to him, makes us love Him even more and gives us a warm feeling of identification with Him. So acknowledging His Mercy is a mercy within itself. SubhanAllah

"Indeed, no one despairs of relief from Allah except the disbelieving people."
(Surah Yusuf, 12:87)

Some Signs Of Allah's Mercy

"Then which of the Blessings of your Lord will you deny?"
(Qur'an 55:13)

THE PROPHETS AND MESSENGERS

Allah (SWT) sent Prophets and Messengers to guide us and help us remain on the right path leading to Jannah.
They all were human beings, sent to different nations, and sent to guide people who had forgotten their Lord, Allah (SWT). They showed the people the best way to live and lead a life that would give them success and happiness in this life and in the next.

Prophet Muhammad (PBUH) was the Last Messenger, sent to all of mankind. He (PBUH) was sent with a universal message for all people, in all places and at all times.

Allah (SWT) says:

"And We have not sent you, [O Muhammad], except as a mercy to the worlds."
(Surah Al-Anbiya, 21:107)

Prophet Muhammad (PBUH) was the embodiment of Mercy. He (PBUH) showed gentleness and compassion to all.

In another surah in the Qur'an, Allah (SWT) states:

"There has certainly come to you a Messenger from among yourselves. Grievous to him is what you suffer; [he is] concerned over you and to the believers is kind and merciful."
(Surah At Tawbah, 9:128)

"So by mercy from Allah, [O Muhammad], you were lenient with them. And if you had been rude [in speech] and harsh in heart, they would have disbanded from about you. So pardon them and ask forgiveness for them and consult them in the matter. And when you have decided, then rely upon Allah. Indeed, Allah loves those who rely [upon Him]."
(Surah Al-Imran, 3:159)

He (sallallahu alayhi wasallam) was so merciful and kind, not only towards his followers, but also towards his enemies and those who had caused him harm. He was a mercy for

believers, a mercy towards his enemies, a mercy for women who were badly treated in them times, a mercy for children and a mercy for animals.
He was sincere and balanced in his love and more compassionate than any other person.
Allah sent him as a source of His mercy upon the Earth.

BLESSINGS FOUND WITHIN US AND ALL AROUND US

Dear brothers and sisters, Look at your body and ponder upon the health you take for granted, the sight, hearing, taste, smell, the ability to touch and move without difficulty.
All these blessings Allah (SWT)has given us that we don't acknowledge as much as we should.
Even if He (SWT) was to cause us to lose one or two of these senses and abilities, we still have so many others that He (SWT) has granted us.
If this isn't from Allah's Mercy upon us what else is.

The Merciful Creator ensures that all His creation is looked after – from the fish in the depths of the ocean, to the insects in the earth, and the birds in the skies.
Everything we have is due to Allah's Mercy. How can a believer not be grateful?
Praise be to Allah, Who possesses all things and who gives without measure.

Allah (SWT) says in the Holy Qur'an:

"It is Allah who made for you the earth a place of settlement and the sky a ceiling and formed you and perfected

your forms and provided you with good things. That is Allah, your Lord; then blessed is Allah, Lord of the worlds."
(Surah Ghafir, 40:64)

"And out of His mercy He made for you the night and the day that you may rest therein and [by day] seek from His bounty and [that] perhaps you will be grateful."
(Surah Al-Qasas, 28:73)

All goodness that reaches us is from Allah's Mercy.
Allah (SWT) has given us day, for us to work hard and do our duties, and He has given us night, for us to rest. He (SWT) has made some animal meat halal for us, which we can eat and enjoy and gain strength with. Granted us fertile land which we can plough and grow crops on and fresh water to quench our thirst and improve the condition of our bodies. All of these things are due to His Infinite Mercy.

He has provided provision for all His creation, even the fish in the deepest darkest parts of the oceans and the smallest insects hidden under rocks and trees. His Mercy surrounds all.

"And cause not corruption upon the earth after its reformation. And invoke Him in fear and aspiration. Indeed, the mercy of Allah is near to the doers of good."
(Surah At Tawbah, 7:56)

Allah (SWT) says in the Holy Qur'an:

"And of His signs is that you see the earth stilled, but when We send down upon it rain, it quivers and grows. Indeed, He who has given it life is the Giver of Life to the dead. Indeed, He is over all things competent."
(Surah Fussilat, 41:39)

And a few verses later...

"We will show them Our signs in the horizons and within themselves until it becomes clear to them that it is the truth. But is it not sufficient concerning your Lord that He is, over all things, a Witness?"
(Surah Fussilat, 41:53)

The fact that Allah has placed so many signs in the world around us, each sign acting as a reminder for us of His Might and Power, is a great Mercy in of itself.
Through these signs it's made much easier for a person to remember Allah and Know of His Existence.

So
"Which of the Favours of your Lord will you deny?"

We weren't left to figure out life and our purpose in this world, by ourselves. Allah granted us guidelines to follow and guides to show us how to succeed. He wants us to succeed!
Hope in the Mercy of Allah should be accompanied by regret and remorse of the heart upon the sins committed, sincerity, and hastening in repentance and avoiding sins. Only then will a person be worthy of it.

RAIN

Rain is one of the great blessings and sources of rahmah of Allah (SWT). In it is life for humans, plants and animals. Without rain, life as we know it would not exist.

As believers, we need to reflect on this great blessing that Allah sends to us. Rain is a great miracle of Allah, a miracle that is often taken for granted and sometimes often detested.

Allah (SWT) says:

"It is He who sends down rain from the sky; from it is drink and from it is foliage in which you pasture [animals].
He causes to grow for you thereby the crops, olives, palm trees, grapevines, and from all the fruits. Indeed in that is a sign for a people who give thought."
(Surah An-Nahl, 16:10-11)

"And it is He who sends down the rain after they had despaired and spreads His mercy. And He is the Protector, the Praiseworthy."
(Surah Ash-Shuraa, 42:28)

The prophet Muhammad (PBUH) used to rejoice when rain fell and one of the beautiful Sunnahs of the Messenger of Allah (PBUH) was to uncover a portion of his body and expose it to the rainfall.

Rain, as it pours over us every once in a while, shows us proof of the existence of Allah, and reminds us of His Mercy and Compassion towards the creation.

There are so many hadith in which rain is mentioned as a blessing from Allah, and the believer is encouraged to make dua and pray when it's raining.

Anas (radi Allahu anhu) narrated,

"We were with Allah's Messenger (PBUH) when rain fell upon us. Allah's Messenger opened up his garment a bit so that the rain could touch his skin. We asked: "O Messenger of Allah, why do you do this?" He replied: "Because it just recently came from it's Lord."
(Sahih Muslim)

The Messenger of Allah (PBUH) said:

"Prayer is not rejected at 2 times, when the call to prayer resounds (adhan) and when it rains"
(Reported by Al-Hakim)

(There is a hadith with similar wording in Abu Dawud, and ibn Majah)

Rain has so many benefits and blessings, all through the Mercy of Allah (SWT).

Imam An Nawawi said:

"The rainfall is a mercy which Allah has just created, therefore use it as a blessing."

It is narrated by Ibn Abbas (may Allah be pleased with him) that once when the rain fell from the heavens, he told his servant to bring out his mattress and saddle so that the rain may fall on it. Abu Jawzaa' then asked Ibn Abbas:

Why are you doing that, May Allah have mercy on you?

Ibn Abbas then said:

"Do you not read the book of Allah: *"And we have sent down from the heavens water that is blessed"* (Qur'an 50:9)…Therefore I would like the blessing to fall (incur) on them."

(From Imaam As Shafii's book, Al-Umm)

'Seek the response to your du'as when the armies meet, and the prayer is called, and when rain falls'

(reported by Imam al-Shafi' in al-Umm, al-Sahihah)

مُطِرْنَا بِفَضْلِ اللهِ وَرَحْمَتِهِ

"We have been given rain by the grace and mercy of Allah."

(Sahih Bukhari, Sahih Muslim)

LENIENCY IN MATTERS OF WORSHIP

Allah (SWT) has granted us such a beautifully easy religion to follow. Islam is compatible at all times, with all people. Even the smallest actions, if done in a certain way are classed as worship.

When a person intends to do a good deed, a good deed is written down just for the intention, whether they go through with actually doing it or not. Then when they do it, an additional good deed is written down. However, when a person intends to do a sinful deed, but does not do it, no bad deed is written down. A sin is only recorded when the person actually commits it.

This is from one of Allah's great blessings upon the believers and all blessings stem from His Mercy towards His creation.

It is through His Mercy that 50 daily prayers were reduced to 5, and fasting was made obligatory for only one month in a year. Even the smallest acts of worship reap huge rewards and small deeds weigh down heavily on the right scale. This is how easy the Deen has been made for the believer.

FORGIVENESS OF SINS

Our Lord Allah (SWT) has given us the opportunity to seek His Forgiveness. By way of His Mercy towards us, He has opened the gates of repentance for us, and commanded us to turn to Him, each time sins overwhelm us.

This is one of the greatest signs of His Mercy upon His servants. Even if a person spends their whole life in sin, if they ask for Allah's forgiveness wholeheartedly, Allah (SWT) promises to forgive them.

Allah (SWT) says:

"And whoever does evil or wrongs himself, but

afterwards seeks Allah's forgiveness, he will find Allah Most Forgiving, Most Merciful"
(al-Nisa' 4:110)

Abdullah ibn Amr reported:
The Messenger of Allah, peace and blessings be upon him, was upon the pulpit and he said:

"Be merciful to others and you will receive mercy. Forgive others and Allah will forgive you."
(Source: Musnad Ahmad)

Although Allah hates sin and warns of punishment for committing them, He does not want His slaves to despair of His Mercy. It was said to Hasan al Basri:

Wouldn't anyone feel ashamed before his Lord to seek forgiveness from his sin, then to go back to it, then seek forgiveness and then go back to it? He said: "Shaytaan would like you to feel that way; never give up seeking forgiveness"

If we didn't have the option to ask for Allah's forgiveness every time we sinned, we truly would be lost and we'd fall in to despair. All praises to The Merciful.

In other verses Allah (SWT) states:

"Will they not turn with repentance to Allah and ask His forgiveness? For Allah is Oft-Forgiving, Most Merciful"
(al-Maa'idah 5:74)

"And He it is Who accepts repentance from His slaves, and forgives sins, and He knows what you do"
(ash-Shura 42:25)

The beauty is that Allah reminds us Himself, again and again to turn back to Him. He doesn't want any of His creation to miss out from His Rahma.

AHADITH ON ALLAH'S FORGIVENESS:

Abdullah ibn Amr reported:
The Messenger of Allah (PBUH) said:

"Allah rejoices more over the repentance of His slave than any one of you who finds his camel after having lost it in a desolate land."

Agreed upon

If it wasn't for Allah's Compassion and Mercy upon his servants, nobody would be able to enter Jannah and free themselves from the wrong they've done. Allah (SWT) waits for His servants to turn back to Him and forgives them when they repent.

The Prophet (PBUH) said,

"He who performs ablution properly, then prays any two

rak'aah (of salaah) without being heedless, will get all his previous sins forgiven."
(Ahmad)

It was narrated from Abu Moosa 'Abd-Allah ibn Qays al-Ash'ari (radi Allahu anhu) that the Prophet (PBUH) said:

"Allah spreads out His hand at night to accept the repent-ance of the one who sinned during the day, and He spreads out His hand by day to accept the repentance of the one who sinned during the night, (and that will contin-ue) until the sun rises from the west."
(Sahih Muslim, 2759)

In another hadith RasulAllah sallallahu alayhi wasallam said:

'Abd-Allaah ibn 'Umar ibn al-Khattaab (radi Allahu anhuma) said that the Prophet (PBUH) said:

"Allah will accept the repentance of His slave so long as the death-rattle has not yet reached his throat."
(al-Tirmidhi)

It is part of human nature that we find ourselves sometimes straying from the path, and committing sins. The difference between a believer and a regular person is that a believer eventually rectifies his/her mistakes by turning to Allah (SWT) and asking Him for His forgiveness.

Merciful Allah loves for his servants to turn back to Him and loves to Forgive. Indeed Allah has made repentance extremely easy for us and He loves the one who repents.

Let us remember that Prophet Adam alayhi slaam was misled by Shaytaan into disobeying Allah. However, he regretted it considerably and repented very sincerely. Allah showed His Mercy and revealed the words for seeking forgiveness from Him.

"Our Lord! We have wronged ourselves.
If Thou forgive us not, and bestow not upon us Your Mercy, we shall certainly be of the losers."
(Al-A'raf; 7:23)

Hence the Prophet (PBUH) said:

"By the One in Whose hand is my soul, if you did not commit sin Allah would do away with you and bring people who would commit sin then pray for forgiveness."
(Sahih Muslim, 2749)

And he (PBUH) said:

""Every son of Adam sins, and the best of those who sin are those who repent."
(al-Tirmidhi, 2499)

Most of us, unfortunately, take Allah's Mercy and compassion for granted and have a lazy attitude towards asking for forgiveness. But if we stop for a moment and just reflect on the depth and extent of Allah's Mercy, we will be astonished beyond words.

SubhanAllah, Allah (SWT) has given us so many signs, so that we turn back to Him. These were but a few signs out of the many. Think about and ponder upon all the blessings Allah has given you and realise the extent of His Mercy upon the whole of creation.

"O Allah, You are my Lord, there is no God but You. You have created me, and I am Your slave. I try my best to keep my covenant (faith) with You and to live in the hope of Your promise. I seek refuge in You from the evil I have done. I acknowledge Your favours upon me, and I admit my sins. Please, forgive me, for none forgives sins but YOU."

(Sahih Al-Bukhari)

THE MAN WHO KILLED 99 PEOPLE

It was narrated from Abu Sa'eed Sa'd ibn Maalik ibn Sinaan al-Khudri (radi Allahu anhu) that the Prophet (PBUH) said:

"There was among the people who came before you a man who killed ninety-nine people. Then he asked about the most knowledgeable person on earth, and was directed to

a hermit, so he went to him, told him that he had killed ninety-nine people, and asked if he could be forgiven. The hermit said, 'No,' so he killed him, thus completing one hundred. Then he asked about the most knowledgeable person on earth and was directed to a scholar. He told him that he had killed one hundred people, and asked whether he could be forgiven. The scholar said, 'Yes, what could possibly come between you and repentance? Go to such-and-such a town, for in it there are people who worship Allah. Go and worship with them, and do not go back to your own town, for it is a bad place." So the man set off, but when he was halfway there, the angel of death came to him, and the angels of mercy and the angels of wrath began to argue over him. The angels of mercy said: 'He had repented and was seeking Allah.' The angels of wrath said: 'He never did any good thing.' An angel in human form came to them, and they asked him to decide the matter. He said: 'Measure the distance between the two lands (his home town and the town he was headed for), and whichever of the two he is closest to is the one to which he belongs.' So they measured the distance, and found that he was closer to the town for which he had been headed, so the angels of mercy took him."

Agreed upon

(NOTE: According to a version narrated by Muslim: *"He was closer to the righteous town by a hand span, so he was counted among its people."*

According to a version narrated by al-Bukhari: *"Allah commanded (the righteous town) to draw closer*

and (the evil town) to move away, and he said:
"Measure the distance between them,'
and he was found to be closer to (the righteous town) by a hand span, so he was forgiven.")

ALLAH'S ATTRIBUTES OF COMPASSION AND MERCY:

• *Al Rahman*	The Merciful
• *Al Raheem*	The Compassionate
• *Al 'Afu*	The Pardoner
• *Al Ghaffar*	The Forgiving
• *Al Ghafoor*	The Forgiving
• *At Tawwaab*	The Ever-Relenting
• *Al Barr*	The Doer of Good

These names all indicate that Allah is characterised by mercy, goodness and generosity. They testify to the vastness and perfection of His Mercy, with which He blesses all of His creation. We can not expect to gain from Allah's Mercy if we do not try to change our errors and work hard to please Him.

Allah says in the Holy Qur'an:

"So if they deny you, [O Muhammad], say,
"Your Lord is the possessor of vast mercy; but His punishment cannot be repelled from the people who are criminals."
(Surah Al-An'am, 6:147)

The above verse tells us that although Allah's Mercy is vast, you need to seek His forgiveness to gain it. A person can not expect to be showered by His Mercy if they are doing nothing to gain it.

ASK FOR ALLAH'S MERCY

My dear, respected brothers and sisters, Make dua Allah (SWT) showers His Mercy upon you and pray for His Forgiveness. Invoke Him using His beautiful attributes of Mercy and you will find Him Most Compassionate, Most Merciful.

One of the ways mentioned in the Holy Qur'an of asking for the Mercy of Allah is as follows:

"Our Lord, grant us from Yourself mercy and prepare for us from our affair right guidance."
(Surah Al Kahf, 18:10)

Ibn Mas'ud (radi Allahu anhu) reported:
"One of the supplications of the Messenger of Allah (PBUH) was:

اللهم إني أسألك موجبات رحمتك، وعزائم مغفرتك، والسلامة من كل إثم، والغنيمة من كل بر، والفوز بالجنة، والنجاة من النار

"O Allah! I beg You for that which incites Your Mercy and the means of Your forgiveness, safety from every sin, the benefit from every good deed, success in attaining Jannah and deliverance from Fire"

O Allah, You are my Lord and I am your slave. I regret all my sins and ask you for forgiveness. Forgive me because only you can forgive. Grant me Mercy as only you can grant Mercy. Ameen.
May Allah accept all of our duas and shower His Mercy upon us.

Allah (SWT) says in the Qur'an:

"And cause not corruption upon the earth after its reformation. And invoke Him in fear and aspiration. Indeed, the mercy of Allah is near to the doers of good."
(Surah Al'Araf, 7:56)

The Messenger of Allah said:

"No one will be saved [from the Hell fire and admitted into Paradise] by his deeds alone.'
When asked, `Not even you, O Messenger of God!', he said,
'Yes, not even me, unless Allah covers me with His mercy. So, do good deeds properly, sincerely and moderately in the morning, in the afternoon and during part of the night. Always remember moderation and always abide by moderation. Thus, you will reach your destination."
(Al-Bukhari and Muslim)

We ask Allah (SWT) to cover us in His Mercy and Forgive our shortcomings. Indeed Allah alone is the Most Merciful.

CHAPTER 4

THE LOVE SONG OF NAMES

I call it, the love song of names
Cause like a song it plays on repeat through my brain

See, I have stumbled and fallen so many times,
My shoulders so heavy from the weight of my crimes
But when I say His name, they feel lighter every time
His name making all my heartbeats rhyme

Tell me, how many times have you cried in the dead of the night?

Felt lost in the world, the air around you so tight
But you've said His name and your burdens felt light
So you said it again, and you felt your troubles take flight

So listen! He's always near, His Love within reach
Whenever you feel weak, just know to Him you can speak

Remember, not every reply is that of speech
Sometimes it comes in the form of the blessings you seek

See I have lain awake at night and whispered His name,

So many times it's become my favourite word game
And with each name, there's so much more love to gain
A love that goes round and round in an everlasting chain

And that's why I call it the love song of names
Cause like a song, it plays on repeat through my brain.

ALLAH'S NAMES

There are 99 names of Allah (SWT), known as the Asmaa ul Husna (the Most beautiful names), and a believer is encouraged to invoke Him using these names.

Each name describes Allah's Beautiful Attributes and they are a means for the servant to know his Creator and gain nearness to Him.

It is a part of human nature that when we love someone, we're eager to find out as much as we can about them. We try to learn all about them and we love to say their name and hear their name spoken in front of us. This is the case of love.

Scholars state that nothing increases one's Imaan more than studying the names and attributes of Allah (SWT), for the more we learn about Him, the more our love increases for Him.

Allah (SWT) has filled the Qur'an with His names and attributes and described His names as 'Husna'.

Husna is the feminine of Ahsan, and ahsan means not just beautiful, not just good, but the very best. The most beautiful. It's not good, it is the best. It's not beautiful, it is the most beautiful Ahsan. There can be nothing more beautiful than Allah's names.

Bear in mind, Allah's names and attributes aren't restricted to only 99. Allah's names are unlimited, but out of all His names these 99 are the Most Beautiful and extra special.

The level of honour of any kind of knowledge has to do with the object of knowledge. Medicine for example is thought of as an elite branch of knowledge as it deals with the human body and it's cures.

Knowledge of Allah and His Names and Attributes is the

noblest and best of all knowledge, because the object of knowledge in this case is Allah, may He be glorified and exalted, through His Names, Attributes and Deeds.

That is why the greatest Ayah in the Qur'an is the Ayaat-ul-Kursi, which consists of the Names and Sifaat of Allah.

As is established in the authentic hadith which is narrated by Muslim from the Prophet -sallAllaahu alayhi wa sallam– that he said to Ubayy bin Ka'ab:

'Do you know which Ayah in the Book of Allah is the greatest?
He answered:
Allah! Lâ ilâha illa Huwa (none has the right to be worshipped but He), the Ever Living [al-Baqarah: 255]
The Prophet -sallAllaahu alayhi wa sallam- patted him on his chest with his hand and said:
'Knowledge congratulates you Abu al-Mundhir'

So this verse of the Qur'an was given honour through the names and sifaat of Allah.

Allah (SWT) says in the Holy Qur'an:

"He is Allah, the Creator, the Inventor, the Fashioner; to Him belong the best names. Whatever is in the heavens and earth is exalting Him. And He is the Exalted in Might, the Wise."
(Surah Al-Hashr, 59:24)

"And to Allah belong the best names, so invoke Him by them. And leave [the company of] those who practice deviation concerning His names. They will be recompensed for what they have been doing."
(Surah Al-A'raf, 7:180)

"Allah - there is no deity except Him.
To Him belong the best names."
(Surah Taha, 20:8)

Throughout the Qur'an Allah (SWT) mentions His Attributes and Names and often a verse ends in one or two of them being mentioned, for example, Tasmiyah is the first thing you read when commencing the recitation of the Qur'an and in it, two of Allah's Names and Attributes are mentioned.

"In the name of Allah,
the Entirely Merciful, the Especially Merciful."

HADITH ON ALLAH'S NAMES

Narrated by Abu Hurayrah (radi Allahu anhu):
Prophet Muhammad (PBUH) said,

"Allah has ninety-nine names, one hundred less one. Whoever learns them by heart will enter Paradise."
(Sahih Al-Bukhari, Sahih Muslim)

"*Learning by heart*" which is mentioned in the hadith, implies the following:

- Memorising them.
- Understanding their meaning.
- Acting in accordance to their meanings.

So if a person knows that Allah is One, he does not associ-ate anything else with Him. If he knows that He is the Provider (ar-Razzaaq), he does not seek provision from anyone other than Him. If he knows that He is Most Merciful
(ar-Raheem), then he does acts of obedience and worship that are the means of attaining His mercy, and so on
NOTE: Memorising them by heart doesn't mean just writing them down and repeating them, rather it means, pronouncing them properly, understanding their meanings and worshipping Allah (SWT) in accordance to what they signify. May Allah grant us all the tawfeeq.

GLORIFY HIM USING THESE NAMES AND ATTRIBUTES.

So he might say:

O Most Merciful
(Ya Rahmaan), have mercy on me; O Oft-forgiving (Ya Ghafoor), forgive me; O Accepter of repentance (Ya Tawwaab), accept my repentance, and so on.

It was narrated that 'A'ishah (radi Allahu anha) said: I noticed that the Messenger of Allah (PBUH) was not in the bed one night, so I looked for him, and my hand fell on the sole of his foot. He was in the mosque, with his feet held upright, and he was saying,

"O Allah, I seek refuge in Your pleasure from Your wrath, in Your forgiveness from Your punishment. I seek refuge in You from You. I cannot praise You enough; You are as You have praised Yourself."
(Sahih Muslim)

The more names and attributes of Allah (SWT) that you use to Glorify Him, the more value your supplication has. For a believer's supplication is beautified by His names.

Maalik ibn Dinaar rahimahullaah said:
'The people of this life they left it and didn't take the best of it,'
they said to him, 'and what is it o Abaa Yahya?'
He said,
'Knowing of Allah The Most Mighty and Majestic.'

99 NAMES OF ALLAH - MEANING, EXPLANATION + RELATED DUA

1. Ar-Rahmaan (The Beneficient)

He who wills goodness and mercy for all His creatures

O Allah, You are Ar-Rahman, Never let us despair of your Mercy, guide us to be merciful to others. We know that your Mercy is perfect.

2. Ar-Raheem (The Merciful)

He who acts with extreme kindness

Oh Allah, you are Raheem. Make us turn to you at all times asking for your Mercy and make us compassionate so that we can enter Your Paradise, by Your Mercy.

3. Al-Malik (The Eternal Lord)

The Sovereign Lord, The One with the complete Dominion, the One Whose Dominion is clear from imperfection

Oh Allah, Guide us in being just in our daily affairs and admit is to your kingdom of Paradise. We know that You are our Only King and Owner.

4. Al-Quddus (The Most Sacred)

The One who is pure from any imperfection and clear from children and adversaries

Ya Quddus, help us in purifying our hearts, deeds, bodies and intentions and aid us in performing the best salah.

5. As-Salaam (The Embodiment of Peace)

The One who is free from every imperfection.

O Allah! Keep us safe in this world and the next, we know that all peace and safety comes from You alone. Keep us safe and grant us peace of heart, body and soul.

6. Al-Mu'min (The Infuser of Faith)

The One who witnessed for Himself that no one is God but Him. And He witnessed for His believers that they are truthful in their belief that no one is God but Him

O Allah, Al– Mu'min, we know that You are the source of faith and Giver of safety, Bless us with strong Imaan and adorn us with all the characteristics of your beloved believers

7. Al-Muhaymin (The Preserver of Safety)

The One who witnesses the saying and deeds of His creatures

Oh Allah. Make us mindful of You in everything we do and aid us in accepting Your decree in good and bad times. We know that You are the One who ensures our well being.

8. Al-Aziz (The Mighty One)

The Strong, The Defeater who is not defeated

Oh Allah, we know that all Might belongs to You, make us among those who rely upon Your Power only and protect us from all those who want to overpower us.

9. Al- Jabbar (The Compeller, The Restorer)

The One that nothing happens in His Dominion except that which He willed

Ya Jabbar, mend our hearts when we are distressed and protect us from oppression and from being oppressive to others

10. Al-Mutakabbir (The Dominant One)

The One who is clear from the attributes of the creatures and from resembling them.

Ya Mutakabbir! Dominate our hearts and fill us with Your love and longing. Grant all those who believe in Your power relief from hardship and keep the pious Muslims dominant over the non believers. No one is like You and no one can answer our prayers but You.

11. Al Khaaliq (The Creator)

The one who brings everything from non existence to existence

O Allah, we know that You are the Creator of all that existed, exists and will exist. Guide us to please You and awaken us to reflect on the Creation. Allow us to ponder upon Your signs in creation and glorify You and praise You.

12. Al-Baari (The Producer)

The Maker, The Creator who has the Power to turn the entities

O Allah, we know that You Create and Form from nothing, guide us to obey You, distance ourselves from bad, and help us to enjoin good and forbid evil

13. Al Musawwir (The Flawless Shaper)

The One who forms His creatures in different pictures.

Ya Musawwir, make us of those who use the blessings You gave us for good, and make us witness the beautiful shapes of Paradise.

14. Al Ghaffar (The Great Forgiver)

The Forgiver, The One who forgives the sins of His slaves time and time again.

Ya Allah, forgive our sins. The first and the last, the hidden and the apparent, the known and the unknown. The sins we have committed knowingly and those we committed unknowingly.

15. Al Qahhaar (The Dominating One)

The Dominant, The One who has the perfect Power and is not unable over anything.

Ya Allah, make us surrender our hearts to You only. Make us ponder Your Power, and help us abandon our sins.

16. Al Wahhab (The Supreme Bestower)

The One who is Generous in giving plenty without any return.

O Allah, Make us of those who are grateful for Your gifts and use them to please You. Allow us to give from what we have to others who are in need. Grant Your favour upon us.

17. Ar Razzaq (The Total Provider)

The Sustainer, The Provider

Ya Razzaq, make us of those who are content with Your Provisions and guide us to work hard to use Your provisions wisely. Grant us grateful hearts and allow us to give from the provision You have granted us, to those who are more in need.

18. Al Fattah (The Supreme Solver)

The Opener, The Reliever, The Judge, The One who opens for His slaves the closed worldly and religious matters.

Ya Fattah, Open our hearts, Open Your door to success. Keep the doors of Your Mercy open for us and allow us to enter through the beautiful doors of Paradise.

19. Al Alim (The All Knowing One)

The Knowledgeable; The One from whom nothing is absent from His knowledge

O All Knowing One, instil in us the eagerness to learn, guide us to the best of knowledge and help us benefit from it.Make us from those who learn and obey.

20. Al Qaabid (The Restricting One)

The Constrictor, The Withholder, The One who constricts the sustenance by His wisdom and expands and widens it with His Generosity and Mercy.

Ya Qaabid, Grant us strong faith to believe that after hardship comes ease. Lead us by Your Withholding to whatever is best for us in this life and the next

21. Al Baasit (The Extender)

The Enlarger, The One who constricts the sustenance by His wisdom and expands and widens it with His Generosity and Mercy

Ya Baasit, We Know that You are the Giver of gifts, make us of those who are grateful for them.

22. Al Khaafid (The Reducer)

The One who lowers whoever He wills by His Destruction and raises whoever He wills by His Endowment.

Ya Khaafidu, You can lower whoever You will by Your destruction, and raise anyone you will by your endowment, make us among the righteous. Do not make us from those who have earned Your Wrath and do not lower us amongst the misguided.

23. Ar Rafi (The Elevating One)

The Exalter, The Elevator, The One who lowers whoever He wills by His Destruction and raises whoever He wills by His Endowment.

O Allah, You elevate people to different ranks, elevate our rank too, when you raise us on the Day of Judgement, raise us amongst the righteous and grant us lofty palaces in Jannah.

24. Al Mu'izz (The Honourer, Bestower)

He gives esteem to whoever He wills, hence there is no one to degrade Him; And He degrades whoever He wills, hence there is no one to give Him esteem.

O Allah! You are the Honourer, grant us honour through Islam and grant us the Honour of gazing upon Your Countenance in Paradise. Grant us the honour of Your pleasure and the honour of being counted amongst the muslimeen.

25. Al Muzill (The Abaser)

The Dishonourer, The One who Humiliates, He gives esteem to whoever He wills, hence there is no one to degrade Him; And He degrades whoever He wills, hence there is no one to give Him esteem.

O Allah! Do not make us from amongst those who You have disgraced. Grant us good companionship and shower Your Mercy and blessings upon us.

26. As Sami (The All Hearer)

The Hearer, The One who Hears all things that are heard by His Eternal Hearing without an ear, instrument or organ.

O Allah! We know You Hear every sound and thought, purify our thoughts and our tongues and make us amongst the righteous. Allow our ears to speak in our favour on the Day of Reckoning. Hear our cries and forgive us

27. Al Baseer (The All Seeing)

The All-Noticing, The One who Sees all things that are seen by His Eternal Seeing without a pupil or any other instrument.

Ya Baseer, we know you See everything; aid us to watch our deeds and use our sight for Your sake only. Make our eyes speak in our favour on the Day of Judgement and keep them from looking at forbidden things.

28. Al Hakam (The Impartial Judge)

The Judge, He is the Ruler and His judgment is His Word.

O Allah! Protect us from the injustice of others, adorn us with reliance upon You and Your justice at all times.

29. Al Adl (The Embodiment of Justice)

The Just, The One who is entitled to do what He does.

Make us of those who are content with your decisions.

30. Al Lateef (The Knower of Subtleties)

The Subtle One, The Gracious, The One who is kind to His slaves and endows upon them.

O Allah! Make us fear You as if we see You, aid us to always be kind and gentle towards others and be patient in hardships.

31. Al Khabeer (The All Aware One)

The One who knows the truth of things.

O Allah You are the One who Knows the truth of things, help us remember Your Watchfulness over us.

32. Al Halim (The Clement One)

The Fore bearing, The One who delays the punishment for those who deserve it and then He might forgive them.

O Allah, protect us from taking advantage of your Hilm by persisting in bad deeds, aid us to turn to You after we sin, and help us to be gentle in times of anger

33. Al 'Adheem (The Magnificent One)

The Great One, The Mighty, The One deserving the attributes of Glory, Extolment, and Purity from all imperfection.

O Allah! Make us glorify You and turn to You in hardship and in ease. Allow us to praise You as much as we possibly can.

34. Al Ghafoor (The Great Forgiver)

The All-Forgiving, The Forgiving.

Ya Ghafoor, You are the Most Forgiving, we call on You to

forgive our sins , hide our faults from others and protect us from the effects of our bad deeds in this life and the next.

35. Ash- Shakoor (The Acknowledging One)

The Grateful, The Appreciative, The One who gives a lot of reward for a little obedience.

O Allah! We know that You are the answerer and fulfiller of prayers; Don't let our prayers be unanswered and adorn us with certainty in Your response. You see our intentions and our efforts, purify them and make us amongst the righteous, deserving of Your favour.

36. Al 'Ali (The Sublime One)

The Most High, The One who is clear from the attributes of the creatures.

O Allah, Al 'Ali , Help us to be humble, to fight our desires and to never place anyone or anything above You. You are The Most Magnificent and Your throne is the loftiest. No one is like You. You alone are our Creator with no partners and sons.

37. Al Kabeer (The Great One)

The Most Great, The One who is greater than everything in status and in every way.

O Allah, Al Kabeer! We know that Your Greatness is perfect and beyond our imagination; Help us to reflect on your Greatness in order to stay close to Your commandments. You can make the impossible, possible, so hear our duas

38. Al Hafidh (The Guarding One)

The Preserver, The Protector, The One who protects whatever and whoever He wills to protect.

O Allah! Help us to fulfil your commands; help us to be mindful of even the smallest of sins and make us rush to repent and be thankful to You for Your protection.

39. Al Muqit (The Sustaining One)

The Maintainer, The Guardian, The Feeder, The One who has the Power.

We know that you are the Only One able to maintain all that ever was, is and will be. O Allah! Sustain our bodies and souls, make us recognise Your Sustenance and guide us to be amongst those who use their sustenance to gain Your pleasure.

40. Al Haseeb (The Reckoning One)

The One who Reckons, The One who gives the satisfaction.

O Allah! Guide us to bringing ourselves to account regularly. You are sufficient for us and the best disposer of our affairs. Raise us amongst the pious on the Day of Reckoning.

41. Al Jaleel (The Majestic One)

The Sublime One, The Beneficent, The One who is attributed with greatness of Power and Glory of status.

O Allah! You are The Most beneficent, The Most Majestic. Forgive our shortcomings and wipe our sins clean. Allow us to be amongst the righteous and let our hearts and minds and tongues glorify You in a manner befitting of Your glory.

42. Al Kareem (The Bountiful One)

The Generous One, The Gracious, The One who is attributed with greatness of Power and Glory of status.

O Kareem! You are the Most Generous, guide us to be generous to others and aid us to develop honourable and noble qualities. All bounties belong to You.

43. Ar Raqib (The Watchful One)

The Watcher, The One that nothing is absent from Him. Hence it's meaning is related to the attribute of Knowledge.

O Raqib! Guide us to be watchful over hearts and our obligations towards You. Help us remember your Watchfulness over us at all times. Allow us to be watchful over our own actions and help us stay firm in our Deen

44. Al Mujib (The Responding One)

The Responsive, The Hearkener, The One who answers the one in need if he asks Him and rescues the one who calls upon Him.

Guide us to respond to your call and be responsive to those in need and make us call upon and supplicate to You in the best manner. You hear and respond to our supplications so grant us a patient heart and firm belief and trust in Your timing.

45. Al Waasi' (The Encompassing)

The Vast, The All-Embracing, The Knowledgeable.

O Allah! Make us of those who constantly remember Your Vastness and Perfection. All things belong to You. You are The One who encompasses all things

46. Al Hakeem (The Wise)

The Wise, The Judge of Judges, The One who is correct in His doings.

O Hakeem! You are the One who possesses ultimate wisdom. Make us of those who are content with Your decisions. Grant us faith in Your timing.

47. Al Wadud (The Loving One)

The One who loves His believing slaves and His believing slaves love Him. His love to His slaves is His Will to be merciful to

them and praise them

O Allah! Make us of those who love You and Your Messenger (PBUH) above all. Grant us firm, ever growing love for our Deen and allow us to love all for Your sake and Your sake alone.

48. Al Majeed (The Glorious One)

The Most Glorious One, The One who is with perfect Power, High Status, Compassion, Generosity and Kindness

O Allah Make us of the dhaakireen (those who remember You continuously with beautiful Glory and praise. Grant us tongues wet with Your remembrance and a heart and mind that praises You continuously.

49. Al Ba'ith (The Infuser of New Life)

The Resurrector, The Raiser (from death), The One who resurrects His slaves after death for reward and/or punishment.

O Allah! You are the Raiser from death, the One who resurrects His slaves after death, for reward or punishment; O Allah! Make us of those raised on the Day of Judgement with our book of good deeds in our right hand.

50. Ash-Shaheed (The All Observing Witness)

The Witness, The One who nothing is absent from Him.

O Allah! We know You witness all things. Guide us to live by the shahada and let us utter the testimony of faith on our deathbed.

51. Al Haqq (The Embodiment of Truth)

The Truth, The True, The One who truly exists.

O Allah! You are the Ultimate truth. Guide us to live and die by the truth and make us of those who advise others to the truth. Don't let us be deceived by Shaytaan and his helpers.

52. Al Wakeel (The Universal Trustee)

The Trustee, The One who gives the satisfaction and is relied upon.

O Allah! We know that You take care of all matters, make us of those who gracefully rely on you. It is You in whom we place our trust.

53. Al Qawwiyy (The Strong One)

The Most Strong, The Strong, The One with the complete Power

O Allah! Make us strong believers and aid us to use our strength to strive for justice. For the sake of your Asmaa 'Al Qawwiyy strengthen our firm and Guide us towards, and keep us firm upon the haqq

54. Al Mateen (The Firm One)

The One with extreme Power which is un-interrupted and He does not get tired.

O Allah! Make us firm in our faith and keep us steadfast in good and bad times. You are the untiring protector of Your creation. Protect us from the traps of shaytaan

55. Al Waliyy (The Protecting Associate)

The Protecting Friend, The Supporter.

O Allah! You are the Most loving guardian; bless us with righteous friends and assist us to turn to Only You at all times. No one loves us more than You.

56. Al Hameed (The Soul Laudable One)

The Praiseworthy, The praised One who deserves to be praised.

O Allah! All praise and thanks belongs to You. Make us of those who praise You as You should be praised.

57. Al Muhsee (The All Enumerating One)

The Counter, The Reckoner, The One who the count of things are known to him.

Oh Allah! You are the Reckoner. The One who the count of

things is known to. Count our good deeds and do not take us into account of our shortcomings. Forgive us.

58. Al Mubdi (The Originator)

The One who started the human being. That is, He created him.

O Allah! Make us of those who hold tight to Your rope, help us gain correct knowledge of the Qur'an and Sunnah and protect us from Bid'ah. You are the originator. There was no life until You Created it. You created everything and brought everything in to existence.

59. Al Mu'eed (The Restorer)

The Reproducer, The One who brings back the creatures after death

O Allah! Mend our hearts when we are distressed and enable us to reach our goals which are pleasing to You. You will restore our bodies on the Day of Judgement and raise us all from our graves. Restore us in a manner most pleasing to You.

60. Al Muhyi' (The Maintainer of Life)

The Restorer, The Giver of Life, The One who took out a living human from semen that does not have a soul. He gives life by giving the souls back to the worn out bodies on the resurrection day and He makes the hearts alive by the light of knowledge.

O Allah! You are the Maintainer, the Restorer, the Giver of life. Put me under Your protection and never leave me alone.

61. Al Mumeet (The Inflictor of Death)

The Creator of Death, The Destroyer, The One who renders the living dead.

Ya Mumeet! We Know that only You are the Creator of Death, do not let us die until You are pleased with us. Give us the strength to read the shahada on our deathbed. Grant us a believer's death.

62. Al Hayy (The Eternally Living One)

The Alive, The One attributed with a life that is unlike our life and is not that of a combination of soul, flesh or blood.

O Allah! Bless us with reliance on You and make us realize Your perfection of Life and so of all Your attributes and guide us to live by them.

63. Al Qayoom (The Self Subsisting One)

The One who remains and does not end.

O Allah! Enable us to practice Qiyaam ul layl often, and grant us actions that bring us closer to You.

64. Al Waajid (The Pointing One)

The Perceiver, The Finder, The Rich who is never poor. Al-Wajd is Richness.

O Allah! You are Al Wajid! The Perceiver! The Finder! Help us find the way to gain Your pleasure and guide us to the straight path of the righteous.

65. Al Maajid (The All Noble One)

The Glorious, He who is Most Glorious.

Ya Maajid! All Glory belongs to You. Help us in understanding and acting upon Your Glorious book and make us of the dhaakireen who praise You night and day.

66. Al Waahid (The Only One)

The Unique, The One, The One without a partner

O Allah! Grant us unshakable belief in Your Oneness and allow us to spread the message of Tawheed far and wide. Save us from falling into shirk.

67. Al Ahad (The Sole One)

The One

O Allah! You are The One who all power belongs to. The only One Creator and Lord of the universes. Forgive us.

68. As-Samad (The Supreme Provider)

The Eternal, The Independent, The Master who is relied upon in matters and reverted to in ones needs.

O Allah! Provide us with halal income and let us live a righteous life. All provision comes from You and You provide for all your creation.

69. AL QAADIR (THE OMNIPOTENT ONE)

The Able, The Capable, The One attributed with Power.

O Allah! We know that Your Power is perfect. Allow us to seek Your forgiveness in abundance. Your Might and Power is everlasting and never fading.

70. Al Muqtadir (The Powerful One)

The Powerful, The Dominant, The One with the perfect Power that nothing is withheld from Him.

O All we know that Your power enforces all decrees, make us grateful for all aspects of Your decree for us. You know best and allow us to have firm faith in Your plan

71. Al Muqaddim (The Expediting One)

The Expediter, The Promoter, The One who puts things in their right places. He makes ahead what He wills and delays what He

wills.

O Allah! Allow us to be patient and grateful to You at all times.

72. Al Mua'khir (The Procrastinator)

The Delayer, The One who puts things in their right places. He makes ahead what He wills and delays what He wills.

73. Al Awwal (The Very First)

The First, The One whose Existence is without a beginning.

O Allah! We know that You are the One without beginning nor end. Guide us to put You and Your pleasure first and foremost. Help us give priority to our prayers

74. Al Akhir (The Infinite Last One)

The Last, The One whose Existence is without an end.

O Allah! We know that You are the Last One who will remain when everything perishes. Bless us with love and eagerness to meet You; enable us to do good deeds who's rewards will continue being counted for us even after our death.

75. Az-Zaahir (The Perceptible One)

The Manifest, The One who has manifest all of creation and who

is manifest in all of creation. The One who is above creation, yet who is made visible through creation.

O Allah! Make both our inward and outward good; guide us on reflecting on Your signs all around us and allow us to praise You.

76. Al Batin (The Imperceptible)

The Hidden, The One who cannot be grasped by our imaginations

O Allah! You know all things, no matter how hidden, how subtle, or how obscure they might be. Make both our inner and outer selves righteous and keep us firm upon Your Love and the love for our Deen. You comprehend all of Your creation and You are near to everything and are intimately aware of all that happens. Grant us all the harmless things we hold secret in our heart and rid us of our insecurities.

77. Al Waali' (The Holder Of Supreme Authority)

The Governor, The One who owns things and manages them.

Oh Allah! You are the Best Guardian. Watch over us and allow us to be amongst those you call Your friends; bless us with goodness in all affairs and grant barakah in our day to day life.

"It is God who has raised the heavens without any supports that you could see, and is established on the throne

of His almightiness; and He it is who has made the sun and the moon subservient to His laws, each running its course for a term set by Him. He governs all that exists."
(Ar-Ra'd 13:2)

78. Al Muta'ali (The Extremely Exalted One)

The Most Exalted, The High Exalted, The One who is clear from the attributes of the creation.

O Allah! Adorn us with firm belief in Your Highness and admit us to the highest paradise without reckoning.

79. Al Barr (The Fountain Head of Truth)

The Source of All Goodness, The Righteous, The One who is kind to His creatures, who covers them with His sustenance and Mercy.

O Allah! Adorn us with the characteristics of the abrar. Make us good and kind and firm upon our belief.

80. At Tawwaab (The Ever Acceptor of Repentance)

The Relenting, The One who grants repentance to whoever He wills among His creatures and accepts their repentance.

Ya Allah! You accept repentance, so accept our repentance and cleanse our hearts. We are sinners but make us from those sinners who repent and stay away from sin. You are The Most Merciful.

81. Al Muntaqim (The Retaliator)

The Avenger, The One who victoriously prevails over His enemies and punishes them for their sins. It may mean the One who destroys them.

O Allah! You are the One who Revenges for the sake of those who are oppressed. Protect the oppressed from the hands of the oppressors. Grant Islam victory and grant us muslims honour and glory. Protect the oppressed muslims all over the world.

82. Al Afuww (The Supreme Pardoner)

The Forgiver, The One with wide forgiveness.

O Allah! We know that You can erase all sins; grant us strength to pardon others so that You will pardon us; pardon all our sins, errors, mistakes and faults.

83. Ar Ra'oof (The Benign One)

The Compassionate, The One with extreme Mercy. The Mercy of Allah is His will to endow upon whoever He willed among His creatures.

O Allah! We know that Your kindness encompasses us, open our hearts to the Qur'an and make us of those who follow Your warnings. What would we do without Your Mercy. Forgive us and cover us in Your mercy.

84. Maalik ul Mulk (The Eternal Possessor of Sovereignty)

The One who controls the Dominion and gives dominion to whoever He willed.

O Allah! Guide us to being responsible on this Earth and make us enter Paradise. Everything belongs to You and You alone. You are the owner of all.

85. Dhul Jalaali wal Ikram (The Possessor of Majesty and Honour)

The Lord of Majesty and Bounty, The One who deserves to be Exalted and not denied.

O Allah! Bless us with the honour of seeing Your Countenance in the Hereafter. Make us of those who you are pleased with and guide us towards the haqq.

86. Al Muqsit (The Just One)

The Equitable, The One who is Just in His judgment.

O Allah! You are Just in Your Judgement. Protect us from the injustice of others, adorn us with reliance upon You and Your justice at all times.

87. Al Jaami' (The Assembler of Scattered Nations)

The Gatherer, The One who gathers the creatures on a day that there is no doubt about, that is the Day of Judgment.

O Allah! We know that You bring together and gather all Creation; make us of those who join and stay with the jam'aa. Guide us and keep us on the straight path.

88. Al Ghaniyy (The Self Sufficient One)

The One who does not need the creation.

O Allah! You need none and all need You; grant us blessings from Your Bounty and make us grateful for all You grant us. You are The only One we can rely on.

89. Al Mughni (The Bestower of Sufficiency)

The Enricher, The One who satisfies the necessities of the creatures.

O Allah! You are sufficient for us; make us of those who are content with Your provisions. You have given us more than we could ever dream of and ask for and You continue to give. Make us of those who praise and thank You always. Do not make us from the ungrateful.

90. Al Maani' (The Preventer)

The Withholder

O Allah! Do not withhold Your blessings from us and our offspring. Shower us with Your Mercy.

91. Ad Daarr (The Distressor)

The One who makes harm reach to whoever He willed and benefit to whoever He willed.

O Allah! Put us beneath the shade of Your Mercy and do not be displeased with us.

92. An Naafi' (The Bestower of Benefits)

The Propitious, The One who makes harm reach to whoever He willed and benefit to whoever He willed.

O Allah! You are the giver of gifts; give us from Your Mercy that overwhelms us in this life and the next.

93. An Noor (The Prime Light)

The Light, The One who guides.

O Allah! All source of light comes from You, fill our graves with lights of Jannah

94. Al Haadi' (The Provider of Guidance)

The Guide, The One whom with His Guidance the living beings have been guided to what is beneficial for them and protected

from what is harmful to them.

Guide us to the right path and Keep us guided

95. Al Badi' (The Unique One)

The Incomparable, The One who created the creation and formed it without any preceding example.

O Allah! Guide us in reviving the ways of your prophet (PBUH) correctly

96. Al Baaqi (The Ever Surviving One)

The Everlasting, The One that the state of non-existence is impossible for Him.

O Allah! Grant us eternal life in the gardens of Paradise

97. Al Waarith' (The Eternal Inheritor)

The Heir, The One whose Existence remains.

Aid us in using our worldly possessions to gain Your pleasure

98. Ar Rasheed (The Guide to Path of Rectitude)

The Guide to the Right Path, The One who guides.

O Allah! Guide us to the right path and towards the path

that leads towards jannah and earns Your pleasure

99. As Saboor (The Extensively Enduring One)

The Patient, The One who does not quickly punish the sinners.

O Allah! We are nothing without Your Mercy, have Mercy on us. You are the Most Merciful.

Each Name and Attribute nourishes a kind of consciousness and humility in man and their study leads one to constantly better their actions.

Allah (SWT) created His creatures to know Him and worship Him. This is what is expected from them and what they are required to do, because as Ibn al-Qayyim (rahemahu Allah) said:

"The key to the call of the Messengers, the essence of their Message, is knowing Allah through His Names and Attributes and Deeds,
because this is the foundation on which the rest of the Message, from beginning to end, is built."

Ibn al-Qayyim (rahemahu Allah) said:

"Knowledge of the Most Beautiful Names of Allah is the basis of all other kinds of knowledge, for the objects of all these other branches of knowledge were either created or commanded by Him (the various branches of knowledge either deal with objects created by Him or with the laws

and guidance revealed by Him). The reason for creation and guidance is found in His Most Beautiful Names (because He is the Creator, He creates things; because He is the Guide to the Straight Path, He reveals guidance, and so on)… Knowing the Most Beautiful Names is the basis of all objects of knowledge, because all knowledge stems from these Names…"

(Bada'i' al-Fawaa'id by Ibn al-Qayyim, 1/163)

Chapter 5

HOT COALS

We're living the days our Prophet peace be upon him foretold,
Days of trials and tribulations increased tenfold.
Holding onto our Deen is like holding onto a hot coal,
Even harder to work towards Jannah, our goal.

So many selling their Deen, for reasons so slight,
Believers by day, disbelievers by night,
So blinded by desires, we're losing our sight,
Darkness of our sins, devouring the light.

Still Allah calls us towards Him, He's always loving,
'Come to me walking, I'll come to you running,
Face me with sins as great as the Earth,
I'll meet you with forgiveness greater in worth.'

The more patience we have, the stronger we get,
Hold firmly onto the rope of Allah, and we have no reason to fret.

Sabr and Shukr is what we need, at all times, in days like these,
Ask for forgiveness, keep on striving, Allah is the One we need to please.
Islam began as something strange, and will revert to being strange,
These are the words of Rasool Allah, that will never change.
So glad tidings to the strangers, who are adhering to the Deen,
On the Day of Judgement, may all our sins be wiped clean.

Ameen

THE AGE OF FITNAH

"Closer and closer to mankind comes their Reckoning: yet they heed not and they turn away."
(Al-Qur'an 21:1)

The holy Prophet (PBUH) was sent to be a role model in all matters, for the whole of mankind, till the end of this temporary world.

Allah (SWT) says:

"And We have not sent you except comprehensively to mankind as a bringer of good tidings and a warner. But most of the people do not know."
(Surah Saba, 34:28)

This means the Messenger of Allah (PBUH) was a bringer of good tidings to the believers; giving them the news of the ultimate reward of Jannah if they adhered to the teachings and commandments of Allah.

He (PBUH) was also a Warner, for he warned the believers about the consequences of their misdeeds and the punishment of Hellfire for those who disbelieve and who commit sins arrogantly, without seeking Allah's Forgiveness.

The knowledge of when Judgement Day will occur, only belongs to Allah (SWT), however it was necessary for the prophet (PBUH) to warn his Ummah about the time of great despair and trials and tribulations that will occur nearing the time of the Last Day, so that they may take heed.

Allah says in the Holy Qur'an:

"Are they waiting for anything except the Hour, to come to them suddenly? But it's Signs have already come!"
(Surah Muhammad, 47:18)

Rasool Allah (PBUH) said:

"As Doomsday approaches, fitnah will increase. It will resemble the increase in darkness as night begins. Many who leave their homes in the morning as Muslims will return home as disbelievers in the evening. While they are Muslims in the evening, they will lose their faith during the night. During such times, staying at home is better than being involved in fitnah. Those who stay aloof are better than those who attack and lead in front. On that day, break your arrows! Leave your weapons! Address everybody with a smiling face and sweet words"
(Abu Dawood)

And

The Prophet (PBUH) said,
"Time will pass rapidly, good deeds will decrease, miserliness will be thrown (in the hearts of the people) afflic-

tions will appear and there will be much 'Al-Harj."
They said, "O Allah's Apostle! What is "Al-Harj?"
He said, "Killing! Killing!"
(Sahih al Bukhari)

Many of these signs have already come to pass. May Allah forgive our shortcomings and keep us steadfast upon the Deen, before it's too late.

DEFINITION OF FITNAH

The word fitna comes from an Arabic verb which means to "seduce, tempt, or lure." There are many shades of meaning, mostly referring to a feeling of disorder or unrest. It is most commonly used to describe trails and tribulations.

Ibn al-A'raabi summed up the meanings of fitnah when he said:

"Fitnah means testing, fitnah means trial, fitnah means wealth, fitnah means children, fitnah means kufr, fitnah means differences of opinion among people, fitnah means burning with fire."
(Lisaan al-'Arab by Ibn Manzoor)

In the Qur'an and the Sunnah, the word fitnah has been used in several ways. In the meaning of trial and testing, blocking and turning away; and in the meanings of shirk and kufr, persecution, falling into sin, hypocrisy and misguidance.

In modern usage, the term Fitnah has been used to describe things that cause controversy, scandal, chaos and discord amongst the Muslim community, disturbing social peace and order. The term has also been used to describe the cultural and religious divisions that occurred in the early years of the Muslim community.

Fitnah is the spread of falsehood that causes a rift amongst the Muslims.

Ibn Al Atheer said:

"Fitnah: trial or test... The word is often used to describe tests in which something disliked is eliminated. Later it was also often used in the sense of sin, kufr (disbelief), fighting, burning, removing and diverting."

(al-Nihaayah)

BELIEVERS BY DAY, DISBELIEVERS BY NIGHT

It has been authentically established that the Prophet (PBUH) said, as part of a longer hadith:

بَادِرُوا بِالأَعْمَالِ فِتَنًا كَقِطَعِ اللَّيْلِ الْمُظْلِمِ، يُصْبِحُ الرَّجُلُ فِيهَا مُسْلِمًا وَيُمْسِي كَافِرًا، وَيُمْسِي مُؤْمِنًا، وَيُصْبِحُ كَافِرًا، يَبِيعُ دِينَهُ بِعَرَضٍ مِنَ الدُّنْيَا

"Rush to perform (good) deeds now, before fitan (trials and tribulations) of pitch-black darkness (appear), wherein a man wakes up as a believer and becomes a disbeliever by nightfall, and another man goes to bed as a believer and wakes up as a disbeliever, selling his Religion for some worldly commodities."
(Sahih Muslim)

This means that the strangeness of Islam will increase to a point where a believer wakes up as a Muslim and becomes a disbeliever by nightfall, or the opposite – he goes to bed as a believer and wakes up as a disbeliever, by selling out his Religion for some worldly gain.

"Selling out his religion for some worldly gain" can mean, formally renouncing one's religion for another because of the temp-tation of wealth etc, or to forgo/compromise a deed of Islam in exchange of some worldly gain.

The trails and tribulations have been described as a pitch black darkness, that no light can penetrate. This could be referring to the blind state people will be in during them days, in regards to their Deen.

The Messenger of Allah (PBUH) urged us to rush towards good deeds now, so that we don't fall in to a state of negligence towards our Deen.

Sometimes apostasy can occur by seeking worldly things and loving this world too much, preferring it over the Next Life and the Akhirah.

When a man's priority is his worldly assets, then to compromise on his religion is not considered serious anymore!

For this reason, we find it has become so easy for people to say and do wrong things just to satisfy certain individuals or to attain wealth, riches and possessions.

Allah (SWT) speaks about those who choose the worldly life over the Deen and the Akhirah, in the Qur'an and says:

"Those are the ones who have purchased error [in exchange] for guidance, so their transaction has brought no profit, nor were they guided. Their example is that of one who kindled a fire, but when it illuminated what was around him, Allah took away their light and left them in darkness [so] they could not see."
(Surah Al Baqarah, 2:16-17)

NOTE: In his Tafsir, As-Suddi reported that Ibn `Abbas and Ibn Mas`ud commented on; (These are they who have purchased error with guidance) saying it means, "They pursued misguidance and abandoned guidance. "Mujahid said, "They believed and then disbelieved," while Qatadah said, "They preferred deviation to guidance."

Allah (SWT) says to them:

"But you prefer the worldly life,
While the Hereafter is better and more enduring."
(Surah Al A'la, 87:16-17)

NOTE (Tafsir Ibn Kathir): 'Rather you prefer the life of this world' meaning, you give it precedence over the matter of the Hereafter, and you prefer it because of what it contains of usefulness and benefit for you in livelihood and your returns.

(Although the Hereafter is better and more enduring) meaning, the reward of the final abode is better than the worldly life and it is more relaxing. For indeed, this worldly life is lowly and temporal, whereas the Hereafter is noble and eternal. Thus, how can an intelligent person prefer that which is short-lived over that which is eternal. How can he give importance to that which will soon pass away from him, while ignoring the importance of the abode of eternity and infinity.

Imam Ahmed recorded from Abu Musa al Ash'ari, that the Messenger of Allah (PBUH) said:

"Whoever loves his worldly life, will suffer in his Hereafter, and whoever loves his Hereafter, will suffer in his worldly life. Therefore, choose that which is everlasting over that which is temporal."
(Imam Ahmed was alone in recording this hadith)

Abdullah ibn Umar reported: We were sitting with the Messenger of Allah, peace and blessings be upon him, and he mentioned several trials until he mentioned a trial in which people should remain in their houses. It was said, "O Messenger of Allah, what is this trial in which people should remain in their houses?" The Prophet said,

"It is evacuation and war. Then there will come a trial which appears pleasant. Its murkiness is due to the coming of a man from my household who imagines that he is part of me but he is not, for my allies are only the righteous who fear Allah. Then the people will gather under a man un-stable like a hip bone over a rib. Then there will be an enormous trial which not leave anyone from this nation unaffected, and just when people say it is finished it will be extended further. During this trial a man will be a believer in the morning and an unbeliever by evening, such that people will be in two camps: the camp of faith without hypocrisy and the camp of hypocrisy without faith. When that happens, then expect the False Messiah to emerge that day or the next."
(Sunan Abu Dawud)

EVILS WHICH WILL BEFALL THE UMMAH DURING THE FITNAH PERIOD, BEFORE THE LAST DAY

Ali Ibn Abi Talib said that the Messenger of Allah (PBUH) said:

'If my Ummah bears fifteen traits, tribulation will befall it.'

Someone asked, 'What are they, O Messenger of Allah?'

He said,

'When any gain is shared out only among the rich, with no benefit to the poor; when a trust becomes a means of making a profit; when paying Zakat becomes a burden; when a man obeys his wife and disobeys his mother; and treats his friend kindly whilst shunning his father; when voices are raised in the mosques; when the leader of a people is the worst of them; when people treat a man with respect because they fear some evil he may do; when much wine is drunk; when men wear silk; when female singers and musical instruments become popular; when the last ones of this Ummah curse the first ones - then let them expect a red wind, or the earth to swallow them, or to be transformed into animals.'

(At-Tirmidhi)

The Prophet (PBUH) gave the ummah signs and described the state the Muslims would be in during the fitnah
period. These are the days we are living in now, as everything that has been described, has come to pass or is happening around us right now.
May Allah (SWT) protect us from such trails, guard our Imaan and keep us on the path of the righteous. Ameen

Abdullah Ibn Umar (radi Allahu anhu) said, that the Messenger of Allah (PBUH) said:

'O Muhajirun, you may be afflicted by five things; God forbid that you should live to see them. If fornication should become widespread, you should realise that this has never happened without new diseases befalling the people which their forebears never suffered.
If people should begin to cheat in weighing out goods, you should realise that this has never happened without drought and famine befalling the people, and their rulers oppressing them.
If people should withhold zakat, you should realise that this has never happened without the rain being stopped from falling; and were it not for the animals' sake, it would never rain again.
If people should break their covenant with Allah and His Messenger, you should realise that his has never happened without Allah sending an enemy against them to take some of their possessions by force.
If the leaders do not govern according to the Book of Allah, you should realise that this has never happened without Allah making them into groups and making them fight one another.'

(Ibn Majah)

---

7 SIGNS OF THE AGE OF FITNAH

People will compete with one another in constructing high buildings
(Bukhari)

Music and Musical instruments will be found in every home.
(Tirmidhi)

Trials will divide the nation (in to sects) and safety will be in adhering to the Al Jamaa'ah
(Ibn Maajah)

Sinking (swallowing) of the Earth, Frequent Earthquakes, flying of stones with severe winds.
(Tirmidhi)

Impact of the tongue is more harsh then the impact of the sword (when people dispute over petty issues).
(Abu Dawud)

Men will start obeying wives More than their mother's orders
(Tirmidhi)

Voices will be raised in Masjids
(Tirmidhi)

PATIENCE AND PRAYER

During these troublesome times, the best way a believer can ensure that they hold firmly to the rope of Allah and that they don't stray from the path of righteousness, is to increase in prayer and stay patient and keep their faith firm in Allah (SWT)

Anas ibn Malik reported, that the Messenger of Allah (PBUH) said:

"The people will see a time of patience in which someone adhering to his religion will be as if he were grasping a hot coal."
(Sunan At Tirmidhi)

Such is the state of these hard times, that everything good that leads to piety will decrease, evil and everything that leads to it will be common, righteous people will be few and the misguided will be many. There will be wide spread trials of misguidance, doubtful matters, indistinguishable issues and rampant atheism.

The people living at this time, will be faced with constant worldly temptations, and these things if succumbed to, will weaken their faith.

We are living these times now. We see it with our very own eyes. The only way we can overcome all these obstacles, is by adhering to the Deen.

Practicing Islam with knowledge and certainty in faith, is the

only way to withstand those trials and temptations. The believer whose faith is firm is the best of creation and is the noblest in the Sight of Allah (SWT).
Allah will help them do the things He loves and help them earn His Pleasure, for indeed help from Allah (SWT) is earned based on a person's faith.

Surrounded by so much darkness of sin and trials of evil, the believer still stays strong and doesn't despair of Allah's Mercy and Help.
Being patient in those times has been described as holding on to a hot coal; staying patient will be very difficult, but in it is success.

Allah (SWT) promised in the Qur'an and He never breaks His promise:

فَإِنَّ مَعَ الْعُسْرِ يُسْرًا

"For indeed, with hardship [will be] ease."

(Surah Ash-Sharh, 94:5)

NOTE: (This promise, Allah made twice right after each other. When speech is repeated, it is often to show the importance of what is being said.
Allah has given the believers the promise that there will be ease after every hardship, and He does so twice. This emphasises His Promise and no one fulfils their promise better than Allah).

And in other ayaat He says:

وَمَن يَتَّقِ اللَّهَ يَجْعَل لَّهُ مَخْرَجًا

"And whoever fears Allah - He will make for him a way out"

وَمَن يَتَوَكَّلْ عَلَى اللَّهِ فَهُوَ حَسْبُهُ

And whoever relies upon Allah - then He is sufficient for him.

(Surah At-Talaq, 65:2-3)

It is reported that Hasan al Basri– may Allah have Mercy upon him– said, when asked 'what is Imaan (faith)?'

It is perseverance (al-sabr) from the things that are forbidden by Allâh the Mighty and Majestic, and acceptance. He was asked, "What is perseverance and acceptance?"
He replied, "al-sabr is to persevere in holding back from what Allâh has forbidden, and [acceptance is] acceptance of what Allâh the Mighty and Majestic has commanded."

GAINING NEARNESS TO ALLAH

In order to gain Allah's help, a believer must earn it, by living life according to what is halal, and staying away from the haram.
The first step to gaining Allah's Mercy and pleasure, is to sincerely repent from all the sins you have committed. The more good deeds you do, the closer you come to Allah. Remember Him and praise, love and fear Him as He should be loved and feared.

Stay away from the forbidden and run towards the deeds and actions that will elevate your status in the eyes of Allah.

WHAT IS MEANT BY REPENTANCE?

Repentance means, returning to Allah, giving up sin and hating it, and regretting falling short in obedience to Allah (SWT). To plead for Allah's forgiveness and to humble yourself in front of Allah acknowledging your sins and being ashamed of your disobedience.

A Muslim's faith may become weak and he may be overwhelmed by his desires. The Shaytaan may make sin attractive to him, so he wrongs himself (commits sin). But Allah is Kind to His slaves, and His mercy encompasses all things.

As long as a believer continues to seek Allah's forgiveness, he will find His Lord to be Most Forgiving.

CONDITIONS OF REPENTANCE

Imam An Nawawi (rahemahu Allah) said:

"Repentance is essential from every sin, even if it is something between a person and Allah (SWT) and has nothing to do with the rights of another person. There are three conditions of repentance:

1- You should give up the sin

2- You should regret having done it

3- You should resolve never to go back to it.

If one of these three is missing, then your repentance is not sincere.

If the sin has to do with the rights of another person, then there are four conditions: the three mentioned above and restoring the rights of that person. If it is money or property, etc, it must be returned to him; if it had to do with slandering him etc, then you should allow him to insult you in return, or ask for his forgiveness; if it had to do with backbiting about him, then you have to ask for his pardon.

It is essential to repent from all sins; if a person repents from some, his repentance from the sins from which he repented is valid – according to the scholars who follow the right path – but he must still repent from the rest as well."

Whoever takes the first steps towards Allah, Allah receives them with His Mercy and makes their path easier towards Him.

Allah's Messenger (PBUH) said that Allah (SWT) said:

"He who comes with a good deed, its reward will be ten like that or even more. And he who comes with vice, his reward will be only one like that, or I can forgive him. He who draws close to Me a hand's span, I will draw close to him an arm's length. And whoever draws near Me an arm's length, I will draw near him a fathom's length. And whoever comes to Me walking, I will go to him running. And whoever faces Me with sins nearly as great as the earth, I will meet him with forgiveness nearly as great as that, provided he does not worship something with me."

(Sahih Muslim, Ibn Majah and others)

Limitless is Allah in His Mercy. The smallest efforts we make towards Him are received with double the reward.

HOLDING FIRMLY TO THE ROPE OF ALLAH

After sincerely repenting and gaining Allah's favour and pleasure, the next step would be to hold firmly on to the rope of Allah (SWT) and to stay steadfast.

'Holding on to the rope of Allah' means to stick to what Allah has commanded and to stay away from what He has forbidden. The rope of Allah being the book of Allah (SWT) and the Sunnah of the Prophet (PBUH).

This Rope is what joins all Muslims together.

Allah says in the Holy Quran:

"O you who have believed, obey Allah and obey the Messenger and those in authority among you. And if you disagree over anything, refer it to Allah and the Messenger, if you should believe in Allah and the Last Day. That is the best [way] and best in result."

(Surah An-Nisa, 4:59)

In another verse He says:

"And hold firmly to the rope of Allah all to-gether and do not become divided...."

(Surah Al Imran, 3:103)

Through these ayah, Allah (SWT) has laid an order out for us. The law being to first listen to Allah (through the Qur'an), then to the beloved Messenger of Allah (through Hadith), and then what is communicated to us by the legal scholars, "those in authority among you"

All these things combined are the rope of Allah.

Imam ibn Kathir, while discussing the meaning of 'the rope of Allah' in his famous book of tafsir, after first discussing the interpretation that it refers to a covenant with Allah, then he brings the explanation that the rope of Allah means the Qur'an.

However scholars have mentioned that the rope of Allah also means;

- Being sincere with Allah
- The whole religion of Islam
- Our Prophet Muhammad
- The pious and upright scholars and the path of the salaf.

"ISLAM BEGAN AS SOMETHING STRANGE..."

The Messenger of Allah (PBUH) said:

"Islam began as something strange and will revert to being strange as it began, so give glad tidings to the strangers."

(Sahih Muslim)

In Sharh Sahih Muslim, Imam An-Nawawi quoted al-Qadi 'Iyad as saying, concerning the meaning of this hadith:

"Islam began among a few individuals, then it spread and prevailed, then it will reduce in numbers until there are only a few left, as it was in the beginning."

Muslim, Tirmidhi and Ahmad and other scholars of hadith, have also collected the above hadith with these added words:

It was said to the Prophet (PBUH)

"Who are they?"

He (PBUH) responded,

"They are those who rectify when the people become corrupted."

In a report transmitted by Imam Ahmad and At-Tabaraanee from the hadith of 'Abdullaah Ibn 'Amr the Prophet (PBUH) said:

The 'glad tidings' is referring to the glad tidings of Paradise). The Prophet (PBUH) said:

"Toobaa is for the strangers."
It was said:
"And who are the strangers?"
He (PBUH) replied:
"A righteous people surrounded by an abundance of evil people. Those who disobey them are more numerous than those who obey them."
(Musnad of Imam Ahmad)

In reference to the times of hardship that were to come the Prophet (PBUH) stated,

"Ahead of you are days of patience, when holding onto the religion will be like holding onto hot coals, and whomsoever holds onto His religion in that time, then his reward will be the reward of fifty men."
The Companions said,
"O Messenger of Allaah, fifty times the worth of their reward?"
He said,
"Rather fifty from you."

Collected by Abu Dawud, At-Tirmidhi, Ibn Maajah, Al-Haakim who declared it authentic

Our faith can get shaken during times of heavy trial, however it is our duty as believers, to remind ourselves that a believer's rank is raised during these times in front of Allah, and that facing these hardships may just well be a sign of Allah's love. Indeed
Allah gives the most tests to His beloved slaves. The reward for being patient during these difficult times, will be like getting the reward of fifty of the sahaba. Subhan Allah. Stay strong.

May Allah (SWT) grant us His Protection from fitan and make us amongst the Ghuraba. May we always remember how fleeting this worldly life is and may we work towards the Hereafter. May our graves be beautiful gardens of Jannah and may Allah's Mercy envelope us always. May we seek solace and protection with Allah's glorious beautiful names and may we stand upright and firm in the face of oncoming trials and tribulations. Ameen

We are nothing without our beautiful Deen! I pray you all stay steadfast and I pray we all pass this test and meet in Jannah.
JazakumAllahu Khayr

Al-Hasan Al-Basree said:

"To endure short-lived difficulties that are followed by long lasting ease, is better than hurrying for a short-lived ease that is followed by ever-lasting hardship."
(Al-Hilyah, 2/134)

يَا مُقَلِّبَ الْقُلُوبِ ثَبِّتْ قَلْبِي عَلَى دِينِكَ

"O, Turner of the hearts, turn our hearts to Your obedience."

About the author.

Zahra Batool is a British born Pakistani muslim, living in England. She is a qualified Aalimah and Qaari'ah, with a masters in Arabic and Islamic studies. She now teaches Islamic studies from home and runs her own two small businesses. Hot Coals, 5 reminders for your faith, is her first book, and she hopes that this book will bring some benefit and be a source of sadqah jaariah for her, and serve as a comfort and reminder for the reader.

Follow her on instagram:

@hotcoals_zahrabatool
@malaabis_mutaanniqa
@zm_canvas_art

Hot Coals

First Edition

ISBN 9781916140745

CPSIA information can be obtained
at www.ICGtesting.com
Printed in the USA
BVHW071955070521
606757BV00005B/623